Vaughn J. Featherstone

THE AARONIC PRIESTHOOD AND YOU

Vaughn J. Featherstone

THE AARONIC PRIESTHOOD AND YOU

Deseret Book Company
Salt Lake City, Utah

This book is not an official publication of The Church of Jesus Christ of Latter-day Saints, and the views expressed in it do not necessarily represent the official position of the Church. The author alone is responsible for its contents.

No part of this book may be reproduced in any
form or by any means without permission in writing
from the publisher, Deseret Book Company,
P.O. Box 30178, Salt Lake City, Utah 84130.
Deseret Book is a registered trademark of
Deseret Book Company.

First printing November 1987

Library of Congress Cataloging-in-Publication Data

Featherstone, Vaughn J.
    The Aaronic priesthood and you.
    Includes index.
    Summary: Explains the significance and responsibilities
of the Aaronic Priesthood in the Mormon Church.
    1. Aaronic Priesthood (Mormon Church)—Juvenile
literature,   2. Mormon Church—Doctrines—Juvenile
literature.   3. Church of Jesus Christ of Latter-day
Saints—Doctrines—Juvenile literature.   [1. Aaronic
Priesthood (Mormon Church) 2. Mormon Church—Doctrines.
3. Church of Jesus Christ of Latter-day Saints—
Doctrines] I. Title.
BX8659.5.F43 1987   262'.149332   87-15731
ISBN 0-87579-085-2

Contents

Introduction

This book is for you, a holder of the Aaronic Priesthood. I hope that your parents and leaders will also find it useful, but mainly it is for you. It will not try to be a complex book about the Aaronic Priesthood. Rather, it is written to help you, who are about to have the Aaronic Priesthood conferred upon you, or who presently serve as a deacon, a teacher, or a priest.

This book explains the basic principles of the Aaronic Priesthood. It tells how it is conferred, who holds its keys, and what its duties are. It describes the brotherhood of the quorum. And it includes chapters on the right conduct, standards, and behavior of young men, and stories about the Book of Mormon, prayer, and worthiness.

It is my prayer and faith and hope that what is contained within its pages will help you grow in stature, wisdom, faith, and maturity, and become one of the great leaders of God's kingdom in the twenty-first century. I see our Aaronic Priesthood young men of today becoming the bishops, stake presidents, mission presidents, temple presidents, and General Authorities of tomorrow.

You, who are now being prepared in the Aaronic Priesthood, may help lead the Church through the most perilous

times in the history of the world. Not only will they be perilous, but they will be challenging and exciting if you keep
the commandments and obey God.

How privileged you are to be, by your own choice, part
of the army of the Lord God of Israel. You have a work to
do, and in the strength and security of our God we will do
it.

Ammon, a prophet of the Book of Mormon, says that
the Lord will protect those who follow him: "They shall not
be beaten down by the storm at the last day; yea, neither
shall they be harrowed up by the whirlwinds; but when the
storm cometh they shall be gathered together in their place,
that the storm cannot penetrate to them; yea, neither shall
they be driven with fierce winds withersoever the enemy listeth
to carry them. But behold, they are in the hands of the Lord
of the harvest, and they are his; and he will raise them up at
the last day." (Alma 26:6-7.)

God's promises are sure. I love to labor in the kingdom.
I love, with everything in my soul, the opportunity I have to
serve. It is not a burden, but a blessing. It is not tiring, but
thrilling. It is not distasteful, but sweet beyond all sweetness.

As you read this volume, may you feel the spirit I felt as
I prepared it. May God bless you, a member of our royal
generation of youth.

Part 1

What Is the Priesthood?

Chapter 1

Commemorating the Aaronic Priesthood

W hat a thrill it is to belong to this church! It is exciting, fulfilling, and glorious beyond description. Every spring, we commemorate the restoration of the Aaronic Priesthood. Can you imagine what would happen if the world believed what we know to be true?

The appearance of John the Baptist to the Prophet Joseph Smith and Oliver Cowdery is one of the most significant events in the history of the world. It will be remembered and talked about in the eternities. Imagine these two young men kneeling in prayer near the banks of the Susquehanna River in Pennsylvania. If people actually believed that during their prayer, John the Baptist appeared to them, the world would change forever. Every honest person in any religion would praise God, weep many tears, and embrace the restored gospel. Consider how that knowledge would change the world. Every knee would bow and every tongue would confess that Jesus is the Christ and that he restored his church in this day.

John the Baptist, by the laying on of hands, holding authority, power, and the proper keys, bestowed the Aaronic Priesthood upon these two wonderful men.

Have you ever wondered what it would be like to see an angel? Think of the sensations that must have pervaded every particle of the souls of these young men. Holy hands were laid upon their heads, and each in turn was given authority. The words of John the Baptist have run down through the last hundred and fifty years. On May 15, 1829, John the Baptist declared in blessing: "Upon you my fellow servants, in the name of Messiah I confer the Priesthood of Aaron, which holds the keys of the ministering of angels, and of the gospel of repentance, and of the baptism by immersion for the remission of sins; and this shall never be taken again from the earth, until the sons of Levi do offer again an offering unto the Lord in righteousness." (D&C 13:1.)

Since that time, the Aaronic Priesthood ranks have swelled to nearly a million. Imagine that number of men and boys endowed with the same priesthood power that Joseph and Oliver received from John the Baptist. Even Joseph at that stage of his life would hardly have dared to believe that from him and Oliver would flow blessings to millions more yet unborn.

It is a marvelous blessing to hold the Aaronic Priesthood. Consider these statements by prophets and apostles. President Wilford Woodruff said: "I went out as a priest, and my companion as an elder, and we traveled thousands of miles, and had many things manifested to us. I desire to impress upon you the fact that it does not make any difference whether a man is a priest or an apostle, if he magnifies his calling. A priest holds the keys of the ministering of angels. Never in my life, as an apostle, as a seventy, or as an elder, have I ever had more of the protection of the Lord than while holding the office as a priest. The Lord revealed to me by visions, by revelations, and by the Holy Spirit, many things that lay before me." (G. Homer Durham, comp., *The Discourses of Wilford Woodruff* [Salt Lake City: Bookcraft, 1946], pp. 298, 300.)

Elder James E. Talmage, who wrote *Jesus the Christ* stated: "I was called and ordained a deacon on Sunday morning, without any previous notice; and that afternoon was placed as a sentinel at the door of the house in which the Saints had met for worship. As soon as I had been ordained, a feeling came to me such as I have never been able to fully describe. It seemed scarcely possible that I, a little boy, could be so honored of God as to be called to the priesthood. I had read of the sons of Aaron and Levi who were chosen for the sacred labors of the Lesser Priesthood, but that I should be called to do part of the service that had been required of them was more than my little mind could grasp. I was both frightened and happy. Then, when I was placed on duty at the door, I forgot that I belonged to the Lord, and that he would assist me in whatever was required of me. I could not resist the conviction that other sentinels, stronger by far than I, stood by me though invisible to human eyes.

"The effect of my ordination to the deaconship entered into all the affairs of my boyish life. I am afraid that sometimes I forgot what I was, but I have ever been thankful that ofttimes I did remember, and the recollection always served to make me better. When at play on the school grounds, and perhaps tempted to take unfair advantage in the game, when in the midst of a dispute with a playmate, I would remember, and the thought would be as effective as though spoken aloud—'I am a deacon; and it is not right that a deacon should act in this way.' On examination days, when it seemed easy for me to copy some other boy's work or to 'crib' from the book, I would remember again—'I am a deacon, and must be honest and true.' When I saw other boys cheating in play or in school, I would say in my mind, 'It would be more wicked for me to do that than it is for them because I am a deacon.' " (*Incidents from the Lives of Our Church Leaders: Course of Study for the Quorums of the Priesthood: Deacons,* 1914 [Salt Lake City: The Church of Jesus Christ of Latter-day Saints, 1914], pp. 135-36.)

And President Kimball shared these thoughts in a conference talk to the priesthood of the Church: "I remember when I was a deacon. (It has been a long time ago, however.)

I thought it was a great honor to be a deacon. My father was always considerate of my responsibilities and always permitted me to take the buggy and horse to gather fast offerings. My responsibility included that part of the town in which I lived, but it was quite a long walk to the homes, and a sack of flour or a bottle of fruit or vegetables or bread became quite heavy as it accumulated. So the buggy was very comfortable and functional. We have changed to cash in later days, but it was commodities in my day. It was a very great honor to do this service for my Heavenly Father; and though times have changed, when money is given generally instead of commodities, it is still a great honor to perform this service.

"I am a deacon. I am always proud that I am a deacon. When I see the Apostles march up to the stand in a solemn assembly to bless the sacrament, and others of the General Authorities step up to the sacrament tables to get the bread and the water and humbly pass it to all the people in the assembly and then return their emptied receptacles, I am very proud that I am a deacon, and a teacher, and a priest.

"In our special meetings in the temple, when the Brethren of the General Authorities come up to the sacrament table to bless, then pass, the sacrament, then my heart beats more audibly again and I am grateful that I hold the sacred Aaronic Priesthood and have the privilege of taking care of the sacrament. Then I remember it was Jesus Christ himself who broke the bread and blessed it and passed it to his Apostles. Then I am proud that I can do likewise." (*Ensign*, May 1975, p. 79.)

From the time Joseph and Oliver were ordained, that process has been repeated millions of times. Young men and adult men have received the Aaronic Priesthood through the laying on of hands. Always the priesthood is conferred first, and then the ordination to the office follows. Once the priesthood has been conferred, it is not reconferred with each ordination. As glorious and marvelous as was the experience for Joseph and Oliver, your ordination is just as glorious. Every young man who has the Aaronic Priesthood conferred upon him has the same power and authority that Joseph and Oliver and John the Baptist had.

The restoration of this great priesthood gives those who hold it more authority in the kingdom of God than all the popes, priests, pastors, and ministers who ever lived. You have greater authority and power than kings, presidents, and rulers of nations. And every young man who has been ordained has that authority and the potential blessing of the ministering of angels.

It is no small thing that this church commemorates the restoration of the priesthood. Over the years I have seen the commemoration celebrated in numerous ways. Many stakes have held track and field meets that included such events as distance races, shot put, broad jump, pole vault, high jump, push-ups, sit-ups, and relays. To bring clean, wholesome young men together to compete is exciting. After the events, the young men receive ribbons for placing in them. From the track meet, the young men return home, change clothes, and go to the chapel for an Aaronic Priesthood banquet where priesthood leaders and guest speakers discuss the power of the Aaronic Priesthood. Here, additional young men may be honored for outstanding achievements in the quorum, ward, stake, or school. Special music is arranged for with young men singing in groups, quartets, or possibly solo. Imagine the thrill of standing in a stake center filled with young men and their leaders singing "A Mormon Boy" or "An Angel from on High" or "I'll Go Where You Want Me to Go." The brotherhood and excitement of such activities are never forgotten.

Some wards and stakes hold sunrise services on a temple lawn, at a historical site, in a secluded canyon, or in a chapel. Every Aaronic Priesthood bearer and prospective priesthood bearer is invited and picked up, and each one participates. Early on a spring Sabbath morning, the song of birds, the sun's rays streaking across the sky, clouds billowing overhead, and a gentle breeze lend to the atmosphere.

Occasionally stakes invite young women to commemorate the restoration of the Aaronic Priesthood, as they also
have an extremely important role in the Church. Young women
and young Aaronic Priesthood brethren dressed in their Sunday best are a beautiful sight. I am confident that the Lord is
pleased and that angels rejoice at such a gathering.

Traditional outings for fathers and sons are nearly always
successful. The brethren of the priesthood gather around the
campfire to sing priesthood hymns and to listen to talks by
young men and their leaders about the restoration of the
Aaronic Priesthood. Then fathers and sons walk together
toward their tents, where the father can share tender feelings
about the priesthood and talk about his youth and quorum
activities.

Service projects are a wonderful way to commemorate
the restoration of the priesthood. Men and boys work side
by side in a widow's yard or at a stake farm or chapel; visit
a care center, hospital, or training school; and so on. Service
is the very heart of the Aaronic Priesthood. All of these activities should be used to strengthen testimonies, activate others, prepare young men for missions, and so on.

Service brings maturity to young men. Years ago I had
the opportunity of traveling to Pocatello with Elder Marion
G. Romney of the Council of the Twelve. I was on the General Priesthood Missionary Committee of the Church. Between
sessions of conference, Elder Romney and I walked several
times around the parking lot. It was a cool, blustery, over-
cast day. As we walked, all of a sudden President Romney
stopped, turned to face me, and said, "Brother Featherstone,
do you think the brethren of the priesthood will ever come
to understand that they were born to serve their fellowmen?"
Everything in my soul responded to that principle. I knew it
was true. The purpose of the priesthood, Aaronic and
Melchizedek, has been, and is, and always will be to serve
God's children here on earth.

We cannot use the priesthood to bless ourselves—but we do receive the promised blessings from God in our faithful service. The priesthood has been given us to bless others.

As we commemorate the restoration of the Aaronic Priesthood, we pay tribute to God for his tender mercies. Only a few of all the souls who have ever walked the earth have held the priesthood. You are one of the elect, the chosen, the ordained of God. As you commemorate the restoration of the Aaronic Priesthood this year, make a commitment to become a true sentinel of God, a servant of your brethren, and a loyal disciple of Christ. Show your reverence for the Aaronic Priesthood in all you do in your home and at school—in athletics, drama, music, Scouting, and in your personal example to your friends. Then you will truly commemorate the restoration of the Aaronic Priesthood.

Chapter 2

You Belong to a Quorum

As we grow up, we usually want to be part of a group, team, or club. The Lord has met that need through the priesthood quorum.

I recall a story of a boy who had lost his mother. His father was a good man, but he didn't talk much—not even to his son. The father provided for the boy's needs, and he loved his son, but he never told him of his love for him. At the age of seven or eight the boy joined a neighborhood gang. They stole cigarettes from one of the boy's fathers and began to smoke. Then they started stealing beer from another father's refrigerator. Soon they were stealing other things.

One day the young man got up and was getting ready for school. His father came into his bedroom. He carried a sign with a string attached to each corner so it could be placed around the boy's neck where all could read it. The sign said, "I AM A THIEF." The father told his son, "If you are going to steal, everyone at school has the right to know that you are a thief so they can watch out for you. You are going to wear that sign to school today, and you are going to wear it all day."

They went in to breakfast, but the boy did not feel much like eating. They ate in silence, and then the father slid the boy's lunch across the table to him and sent him off to school. As lonely as we ever are in this life, the boy walked out the door, down the sidewalk, and then down the street to the corner. He stopped and thought. He knew he couldn't go to school wearing the sign. And he couldn't go back home, so he decided he would run away. He was thinking about where he would go when he heard footsteps behind him. It was his father. His father said to him, "Son I will let you take off the sign if you will make me a promise."

The boy said he would do almost anything to get the sign off. "What is it?" he asked.

"Will you go to Sunday School with me on Sunday?"

They went to church on Sunday. The father went to the adult class. The boy was taken by a Sunday School leader to his class. They opened the door and went in. The class was just starting. The leader said, "This is a new member of your class. Please make him welcome, love him, and let him know we care." The teacher knelt down in front of the boy, put her arms around him, and hugged him. That was the first time he had been hugged and loved since his mother died. He became part of that group. It was a Sunday School group instead of a neighborhood gang.

The Lord has provided a group for every member of his church, and for you it is your priesthood quorum. How do you become a member of a quorum? You start by receiving the priesthood under the direction of the Bishop. If you do not yet hold the priesthood, the person who ordains you will call you by name. Then in the name of Jesus Christ (whose church this is) and by the authority of the Aaronic Priesthood (if the person performing the ordinance is a priest) or the Melchizedek Priesthood, he will confer upon you the Aaronic Priesthood with all of its rights, authorities, and blessings. He will then ordain you to the office of a deacon and give you a blessing.

You should listen carefully to your blessing and remember as much of it as you can. The person who ordains you can receive revelation and inspiration to help you. You can receive the blessings he promises if you live worthy of them.

When I was ordained a deacon, I thought no other boy in the Church was tempted more than I was. When my older brother was ordained a teacher on that same day, the person ordaining him said in the blessing, "I promise you power to overcome temptation." My whole soul responded to that promise.

I remember praying silently, "Heavenly Father, please give me power to overcome temptation. I need it more than my brother."

When I was ordained a deacon I was not told that I would have the power to overcome temptation. I thought, "The Lord knows that I am weak and my brother is strong," and I supposed that I did not deserve that power.

Some time later I read in the Bible these words: "There hath no temptation taken you but such as is common to man: but God is faithful, who will not suffer you to be tempted above that ye are able; but will with the temptation also make a way to escape, that ye may be able to bear it." (1 Corinthians 10:13.)

Then I knew that all people, in or out of the Church, have the promise that God will not permit Satan to tempt them more than they can withstand.

Once you hold the Aaronic Priesthood, the offices of teacher and priest come by ordination, but you are not given the priesthood again since you already hold it.

Deacons, teachers, and priests are all necessary, and all have certain duties. As a deacon, you can pass the sacrament and collect fast offerings, for example. As a teacher, you can also prepare the sacrament. As a priest, you can bless the sacrament; ordain deacons, teachers, and other priests; and perform the ordinance of baptism into the Church.

But no matter which group you belong to, you will always be part of a priesthood quorum. The quorum president will present your name to the members of the quorum and call for a vote to receive you into the quorum. The members will raise their right hands to do this. From then on, you will never belong to a more important group. Belonging to political or worldly organizations is a great honor, but you must be called of God and accepted by your brethren to belong to a quorum in the priesthood of God.

Each quorum has a president. The president is not elected by other members of the quorum; he is called by the Lord through the bishop or branch president. The bishop will interview the young man for worthiness and availability and to see if he is willing to faithfully serve his brethren in the quorum. He will explain the duties of the calling. Then he will call the young man to serve as the president of the quorum.

The new president will prayerfully choose two counselors and recommend them to the bishop to be called. They may or may not be his close friends. If the bishop approves of the counselors, he or his counselor will interview and call them.

The bishop is the president of the Aaronic Priesthood in the ward. He also serves as president of the priests quorum. He interviews and calls his own assistants.

A quorum is instructed and trained by the quorum president. Also, an adviser (who is a member of the ward Young Men presidency) is called by the bishop or branch president to help with the training and instruction. The quorum adviser is accountable to the bishopric. He not only teaches, instructs, and trains quorum members, but he is also involved in all their activities.

The president of the quorum should have a good relationship with the adviser. If the president feels that a particular lesson should be taught, he should counsel with the adviser about it. For example, if the president is worried that some of the quorum members are cheating at school, he might counsel the adviser to discuss honesty during the lesson.

The adviser might also accompany the quorum president or presidency as he visits the boys who are not attending priesthood meeting. Imagine the authority that a quorum president has! This authority is from God. Many in the outside world would hardly believe the responsibilities this young man has; nor would they ever understand the authority every priesthood holder has.

To this day I remember the responsibility I felt as president of my deacons and teachers quorums. The opportunity to serve taught me a great lesson. Years later, when I was a priest, I was nominated as a candidate for the new student-body president of our high school. The four finalists were interviewed by the old president. I will never forget the first question he asked me: "Why do you want to be the student-body president?" I remembered how I had felt about being a quorum president and then answered: "A student-body president is a leader, and a leader serves the people. I love all of you, and I can show my love through my service."

In your quorum, you will be able to serve others. You will reach down to lift other young men who will also serve in the quorum once they have the vision of what God would have them do. Together, you will accomplish a work no other generation has ever accomplished. You will draw close to the Lord, because he has not called you only to leave you without his guidance. You will associate with men of substance. These leaders will have unbending testimonies. They will train you for your foreordained role in the kingdom of God.

They will be your close friends. You will camp together, play together, kneel in prayer together, and serve together. You will visit widows, orphans, and inactive members together. You will come to appreciate the integrity of these men. You will see that they are men of substance, men after whom you could pattern your life. They will be free from the evils of the day. They will live the Word of Wisdom, be clean in their speech, treat women with dignity and respect, honor motherhood, pay their tithing, attend the temple, magnify their priesthood, and serve the Lord. These are the kind of men you will want to use as models.

It is a sacred privilege to belong to a priesthood quorum in The Church of Jesus Christ of Latter-day Saints. Learn your quorum duties and fill them faithfully. The Lord has said to every priesthood holder: "Let every man learn his duty, and to act in the office in which he is appointed, in all diligence. He that is slothful shall not be counted worthy to stand, and he that learns not his duty and shows himself not approved shall not be counted worthy to stand." (D&C 107:99–100.)

Chapter 3

The Glory of Aaronic Priesthood Work

When Jesus visited the Nephites after his resurrection, he invited them to come to him and feel the prints of the nails in his hands and feet and the spear wound in his side. He taught them and left them, with a promise that he would return the next day.

But the people did not go home and sleep. We read in the Book of Mormon, "All the night it was noised abroad concerning Jesus; and insomuch did they send forth unto the people that there were many, yea, an exceedingly great number, did labor exceedingly all that night, that they might be on the morrow in the place where Jesus should show himself unto the multitude." (3 Nephi 19:2-3.)

Out of love, those who had seen the Savior worked all night to spread the word that he would visit them again the next day. He had promised that he would, and his promises are sure. There was no question that he would return. So, all night the people told others to gather to see and hear the Savior.

When we are filled with this same love as Aaronic Priesthood holders, we too will work hard to bring other members of our quorums, our families, and others to Christ so that they may come and partake of the fruit of the gospel.

As the Lord told Thomas B. Marsh through the Prophet Joseph Smith, "Lift up your heart and rejoice, for the hour of your mission is come; and your tongue shall be loosed, and you shall declare glad tidings of great joy unto this generation." (D&C 31:3.)

Doing the Lord's work is a joy. Every young man ought to rejoice when "the hour of [his] mission is come." It is the greatest work you will do. Missionary work is difficult, exciting, and wonderful and brings great joy.

No wonder the people labored all night to make sure that no one was left out. Perhaps even those who were not very excited about the church came in great numbers. I can imagine that many came who seldom prayed, who were selfish, and even who had sinned greatly. But when they came, marvelous things happened to them. None of them were ever the same again.

The first day of his visit, the Lord taught the people that those who sinned should not be cast out, but that they should be helped. Perhaps this teaching is what motivated the people to work so hard throughout the night.

On the second day, the people were taught to pray for the Holy Ghost, and they were given the Holy Ghost so that they would know what to pray for.

✝ As an Aaronic Priesthood holder, you too should pray for the Holy Ghost to be with you, and you should live so that the Holy Ghost will be with you. The Holy Ghost will teach you what to pray for, and as you pray, you will find your heart turning toward purity, service, love, and surrender to the Master's purposes. When this occurs, glorious things will happen to you. The Lord will use you to do his work, and the work you do will be larger than yourself.

The Lord said he would take the weak things of the earth and make them great. It does not matter what handicaps or weaknesses you have, because if you are worthy, the Lord can and will use you to fulfill his purposes.

Most of us feel inadequate. We wonder if we can ever do anything that will be of much worth or importance. Even the great prophet Enoch felt this way. We read in the Pearl of Great Price that Enoch was journeying in the land, among the people; and as he journeyed, the Spirit of God descended out of heaven, saying: "Enoch, my son, prophesy unto this people, and say unto them—Repent. . . . And when Enoch had heard these words, he bowed himself to the earth, before the Lord, and spake before the Lord, saying: Why is it that I have found favor in thy sight, and am but a lad, and all the people hate me; for I am slow of speech; wherefore am I thy servant?" (Moses 6:26-27, 31.)

The Lord knew who Enoch was and what he was fore-ordained to do. And in these thrilling words he gave Enoch a vision of what he would become: "Go forth and do as I have commanded thee, and no man shall pierce thee. Open thy mouth, and it shall be filled, and I will give thee utterance, for all flesh is in my hands, and I will do as seemeth me good. Say unto this people: Choose ye this day, to serve the Lord God who made you. Behold my Spirit is upon you, wherefore all thy words will I justify; and the mountains shall flee before you, and the rivers shall turn from their course; and thou shalt abide in me, and I in you; therefore walk with me." (Moses 6:32-34.)

Moses, too, felt himself inferior to others. He exclaimed, "O my Lord, I am not eloquent, . . . but I am slow of speech, and of a slow tongue." (Exodus 4:10.)

The Lord told Moses that with Him all things are possible: "The Lord said unto him, Who hath made man's mouth? or who maketh the dumb, or deaf, or the seeing, or the blind? have not I the Lord? Now therefore go, and I will be with thy mouth, and teach thee what thou shalt say." (Exodus 4:11-12.)

On the day that our prophet was born, who would have supposed that one day he would lead this church with a mighty ministry? He has sat with kings and presidents and rulers of nations. He has walked humbly with his God and now presides as prophet, seer, and revelator and president of the church of Jesus Christ.

When those who are now General Authorities of the Church were young men in the Aaronic Priesthood, probably none of them supposed that they would walk in such high places when they were older. One of the most unusual of their stories is my own. If someone had told the leaders of my ward that one of their boys would someday be a General Authority, they would never have guessed that I would be the one, nor would I have guessed it.

You all have a work to do, and you must prepare for that work. You may have been foreordained to serve as a bishop, a high councilor, a stake or mission president, a temple president, or a General Authority.

Only the Lord knows whom he will call to be his leaders. Who knows what great work you may be called to do? Who knows what great leaders you may work with in building the kingdom of God?

It is a privilege to serve the Lord, but can you imagine what it would be like to associate with him personally? When he visited the Nephites, he did return to them the second day as he had promised. On that day, the people were filled with the Holy Ghost and with fire. "Behold, they were encircled about as if it were by fire: and it came down from heaven, and the multitude did witness it, and did bear record; and angels did come down out of heaven and did minister unto them. And it came to pass that while the angels were ministering unto the disciples, behold, Jesus came and stood in the midst and ministered unto them." (3 Nephi 19:15.)

Imagine the thrill of those who had not been with him the previous day. Now they were in his presence, and they prayed with him. The Savior's prayer for them must have thrilled them beyond expression.

Through my calling, I have been privileged to associate with great people. Imagine what it would be like to be in the presence of all the General Authorities, including the twelve

apostles and the First Presidency, in an upper room in the
Salt Lake Temple. Consider what it would be like to be in
our training meetings in the Church Administration Building. Can you comprehend what it would be like to sit in
council meetings with stake presidencies and bishoprics each
week?

As glorious as these experiences are, they are not the
most spiritual experiences I have had. The Lord reserves special spiritual experiences for those who minister to the poor,
the orphan, the widow, or to anyone else in difficulty.

I remember meeting with just a few people in a dingy
hospital room in Samoa. A wonderful sister missionary was
dying of cancer in that room, and those of us who were
there felt the presence of unseen beings. This dear woman is
now buried on a small hill in an inconsequential grave, but
the ground where she is buried is holy.

I have been in the homes of the widowed, the poor, the
inactive, the lonely, the sad, and there I have felt the Lord's
presence in ways that are beyond expression. At times, as I
have taught people about the Church, or as I have borne my
testimony, I have felt as if my soul were on fire.

We do not need to serve in the highest councils of the
Church to feel the Spirit of the Lord. His Spirit rests upon us
when we have been greatly tempted but have overcome. It is
with us when we serve in our priesthood callings. It comes
when we quietly study the scriptures or pray in our moments
of despair.

Miracles occur and lives are changed as we fulfill our
priesthood callings. We need to care about people, just as a
shepherd cares about his sheep. And you, my dear Aaronic
Priesthood brother, can have this feeling as you love and
serve the people around you.

The Savior loves every person on earth. Those who break
his commandments also break his heart and injure his tender
feelings. And those who follow in his steps, keep his commandments, and serve others bring inexpressible joy to him.

Consider this beautiful description of what happened to the Nephites who loved the Savior: "When Jesus had . . . prayed unto the Father, he came unto his disciples, and behold, they did still continue, without ceasing, to pray unto him; and they did not multiply many words, for it was given unto them what they should pray, and they were filled with desire. And it came to pass that Jesus blessed them as they did pray unto him; and his countenance did smile upon them, and the light of his countenance did shine upon them, and behold they were as white as the countenance and also the garments of Jesus; and behold the whiteness thereof did exceed all the whiteness, yea, even there could be nothing upon earth so white as the whiteness thereof. . . . And it came to pass that he went again a little way off and prayed unto the Father; and tongue cannot speak the words which he prayed, neither can be written by man the words which he prayed. (3 Nephi 19:24-25, 31-32.)

I hope that you will love the Savior, walk in his paths, and commit your life to him. Greater things will happen in this generation than have ever happened before! Prepare to meet the Savior, for if you do, you shall meet him at his glorious coming.

Chapter 4

Your Priesthood Lineage

President Harold B. Lee said this about the programs
for young people in the Church: "No topic . . .
has received longer and more searching, prayerful
discussion by the General Authorities of the Church
than the matters that pertain to the young people of the
Aaronic Priesthood groups, and the women of similar ages."

He went on to say, "What is intended . . . is that the
programs will go forward, but with priesthood identity the
like of which they have not enjoyed before. And we sincerely
believe that . . . many of those who have not been active
will now be brought into activity: and the priesthood and
the youth . . . will now, under their great leaders, move forward. We hope there will not one be missed. And everybody
will be taken into focus by the great plan of salvation." It
takes this kind of vision to lift the Church and the young
men of the Aaronic Priesthood.

In 1903, President Joseph F. Smith said. "There is no
office growing out of the priesthood that is or can be greater
than the priesthood itself. It is from the priesthood that the
office derives its authority and power. No office gives authority

to the priesthood, but all offices in the Church derive their authority from the priesthood."

The Lord has provided a principle for our guidance as we work in the priesthood: "If your eye be single to my glory, your whole bodies shall be filled with light, and there shall be no darkness in you; and that body which is filled with light comprehendeth all things. Therefore, sanctify yourselves that your minds become single to God, and the days will come that you shall see him; for he will unveil his face unto you, and it shall be in his own time, and in his own way, and according to his own will." (D&C 88:66-68.)

This is similar to the counsel that the Apostle Paul gave to Timothy, who was a young man, perhaps much like you: "Let no man despise thy youth; but be thou an example of the believers, in word, in conversation, in charity, in spirit, in faith, in purity. Till I come, give attendance to reading, to exhortation, to doctrine. Neglect not the gift that is in thee, which was given thee by prophecy, with the laying on of hands. . . . Meditate upon these things; give thyself wholly to them; that thy profiting may appear to all." (1 Timothy 4:12-15.)

Paul's instructions are also important to you. Notice that he advises Timothy to "give attendance to reading, to exhortation, to doctrine"—that is, to understanding the gospel. He wanted Timothy to have his own testimony of the truth, and this is important for you, too. Then when you are confronted with apostasy and false doctrine, you will not be confused and led astray.

It is also important for you to understand that the priesthood you hold can be traced back to Joseph Smith, who received the same priesthood from John the Baptist. Once you know that, you will never doubt that you do hold true priesthood authority. In 1831, the Lord told Joseph Smith: "It shall not be given to any one to go forth to preach my gospel, or to build up my church, except he be ordained by some one who has authority, and it is known to the church that he has authority and has been regularly ordained." (D&C

42:11.) This is how you received your priesthood authority. Elder John Widtsoe wrote: "Every man who holds the [Aaronic] priesthood may trace his authority . . . back to John the Baptist. . . . The chain must be unbroken and the call to the priesthood must have come through the proper authority." (*Priesthood and Church Government*, p. 29.)

In ancient times, 4,289 faithful priesthood holders left Babylon to return to build up Jerusalem. Others claimed to have the priesthood, but they could not prove their priesthood lineage. So, when they returned to Jerusalem, they were not permitted to function in the priesthood. (See Ezra 2:62-63; Nehemiah 7:64-65.)

Through the ages, a person's authority has always depended on his priesthood lineage. This is true throughout the Church. The keys to bestow the priesthood are held by the presiding high priest in your ward (your bishop) and by the presiding high priest in your stake (your stake president). They received their authority from the Quorum of the Twelve and the First Presidency.

Remember that you can trace your authority back to John the Baptist, who appeared to Joseph Smith and Oliver Cowdery and gave them the Aaronic Priesthood. They gave the priesthood to others, who gave it to others, until finally it came to you.

Now that you hold the Aaronic Priesthood, you should learn your duty and prepare for a lifetime of service to the Lord. Nothing else on earth compares to the blessings that come from helping others through the priesthood. The priesthood you hold will bring you the sweetest fulfillment you will ever have.

Money, power, and influence in the world are as nothing when compared to the blessings of the priesthood. Prepare yourself to serve through study, prayer, and faithfulness, and you will be blessed beyond your imagination.

Part 2

The Aaronic
Priesthood Holder

Chapter 5

Prayer and the Aaronic Priesthood Holder

Have you ever wondered what it would be like to hear a prophet of the Lord pray? Imagine what it would be like to hear the Lord Jesus Christ pray. Not only is prayer a great privilege, but we are commanded to pray. Prayer will be very important to you as you carry out your duties in the Aaronic Priesthood.

Not praying about your Aaronic Priesthood assignments would be like playing on a high-school team without ever taking time to talk with the coach. The priesthood is the power of God. It is used to create worlds, heal the sick, raise the dead, and preach the gospel. Because it is God's power, it is impossible to use it correctly without guidance from God. This guidance comes through prayer.

Years ago, my son Dave was home alone. At the time, he was a deacon. The phone rang, and he answered it. The person calling was a dear friend of my wife, and her car had a flat tire. She didn't know how to fix it or who else to call. Dave said, "I'll come change your tire. I know how to do it." He hung up the phone and got his bike. Then he realized that he hadn't asked where she was. He felt obligated to help her, though, because he had said he would. He prayed that

27

Heavenly Father would lead him to this woman. Then he climbed on his bike and rode directly to where she was. He was led by the Spirit because he was trying to do what was right. In the same way, Heavenly Father will answer your prayers as you do your best to fulfill your priesthood responsibilities.

Often we do not understand how near our Heavenly Father really is. Just think: You pray to a God who knows all things, who has all power, and who is concerned about every person. And yet to talk to him you don't have to get past security guards, locked doors, or secretaries. You can talk with him at any time and at any place, whether you are kneeling at your bedside, walking down the street, or standing in a crowded elevator.

When you can, you should find a private spot, kneel, bow your head, and close your eyes to pray. But when you can't do that, you can still let your heart be drawn out in prayer continually, no matter where you are or what you are doing.

The Book of Mormon prophet Alma counseled the Zoramites with great authority and wisdom: "May God grant unto you, my brethren, that ye may begin to exercise your faith unto repentance, that ye begin to call upon his holy name, that he would have mercy upon you; yea, cry unto him for mercy; for he is mighty to save. Yea, humble yourselves, and continue in prayer unto him. Cry unto him when ye are in your fields, yea, over all your flocks. Cry unto him in your houses, yea, over all your household, both morning, mid-day, and evening. Yea, cry unto him against the power of your enemies. Yea, cry unto him against the devil, who is an enemy to all righteousness. Cry unto him over the crops of your fields, that ye may prosper in them. But this is not all; ye must pour out your souls in your closets, and in your secret places, and in your wilderness. Yea, and when you do not cry unto the Lord, let your hearts be full, drawn out in prayer unto him continually for your welfare, and also for the welfare of those who are around you." (Alma 34:17-27.)

Think of how many righteous Aaronic Priesthood holders have stood on a basketball court while the national anthem was being played and offered a silent prayer: "Please, dear God, help me do my best tonight." Imagine how many musicians, teachers, and speakers have offered a simple, silent prayer just before they were called upon to perform. There is great power in doing so.

How could God better show his love for you than to be available twenty-four hours a day, every day of your life? Unfortunately, some do not believe in him. Others have turned in anger from his ways. Still others believe in him but simply act as if he didn't exist, unless they are in trouble—then they call upon him. A poet wrote:

> You might as well pray to a God of stone
> As offer to the living God a prayer of words alone.

Great things come about through prayer. Through prayer, Nephi had angels appear to him. Through prayer, he saw the Lord. Through prayer, he was carried away in vision. When his brothers didn't understand these things, he asked them, "Have ye inquired of the Lord?" (1 Nephi 15:8.)

Nephi also wrote: "My beloved brethren, I perceive that ye ponder still in your hearts; and it grieveth me that I must speak concerning this thing. For if ye would hearken unto the Spirit which teacheth a man to pray ye would know that ye must pray; For the evil spirit teacheth not a man to pray, but teacheth him that he must not pray. But behold, I say unto you that ye must pray always, and not faint; that ye must not perform any thing unto the Lord save in the first place ye shall pray unto the Father in the name of Christ, that he will consecrate thy performance unto thee, that thy performance may be for the welfare of thy soul." (2 Nephi 32:8-9.)

Nephi said of his people, "I pray continually for them by day, and mine eyes water my pillow by night, because of them; and I cry unto my God in faith, and I know that he will hear my cry." (2 Nephi 33:3.) We all have someone to pray for continually. Mothers often pray with broken hearts for sons who have abandoned the teachings of the church. It gives me great strength to know that my mother is praying for me.

I came to understand the power of prayer as an Aaronic Priesthood holder. The junior prom was coming up, and I had asked a lovely girl named Merlene (who later became my wife) to go with me. The problem was, I had no money for the dance, and as the day of the dance grew nearer and nearer, I became more and more desperate. My mom and dad were divorced, and my mom had very little money. I asked her if I could borrow some money to go to the dance and to buy Merlene a corsage, but she simply did not have any money to lend me. I had no one to go to but the Lord. I prayed fervently that I would have the money I needed. Then, the day before the dance, I received a small return on my income tax that was just enough and a little to spare. You might think that this was a coincidence, but I do not. I know the Lord blessed me. And I would rather trust in the Lord than in coincidence.

The Lord will answer your prayers. Be patient, have faith, and prepare to do whatever the Lord's will may be. Two missionaries, Truman G. Madsen and Reuel J. Bawden, once had a wonderful experience with prayer on Prince Edwin Island in the New England mission. Elder Madsen tells the story:

> It was hot and dusty along that country road. "We're about due for something to eat, don't you think?" said Reuel J. Bawden, pretending he'd had a brilliant new thought.
>
> "Huh!" was all that I could manage in reply.
>
> The thought wasn't a new one. Twenty-four hours had passed since we had eaten anything, and our strength was beginning to wane as we trudged along the sparsely populated back road. Latter-day Saint missionaries were rather unpopular with these farm folk, I reflected. We'd been forced to sleep in a barn the night before, and now, at 2 o'clock in the afternoon, we had yet to manage something to eat.

Noticing a clump of trees, I said, "Well, let's go tell the Lord about it."

This happened often in our country work . . . going off into the woods to pray. It wasn't a habit—it was necessity. Who but the Lord could help us in these hostile country areas? We were without purse or scrip. We were on our own. But He in whose work we were engaged was ever within reach, the unfailing resource.

We found a secluded spot, grounded our suitcases with a sigh of relief, and knelt down. Elder B. prayed. It wasn't a long prayer; they seldom were in this work. Forgotten were well-worn phrases and repetitions. We were praying for urgent needs. It didn't take long to express them.

"Father, wilt thou open the way for us to have a bite to eat."

My "Amen" was heartfelt.

As we stood and donned our hats, I noticed a ripple in the small brooklet that gurgled through the grove. A trout rose to strike at a fly. I smiled.

"Oh, for a fishing pole!" I said, half aloud.

"What's wrong with what you have in your hand?" said Elder B.

I looked down at the tattered umbrella and chuckled.

Elder B. wasn't smiling.

"Hmm," he said, "you've got thread; I've got a safety pin; and we ought to be able to find a worm around and—"

A handy man was Elder B. In a few minutes he had doubled and redoubled enough thread to make a line. Then with his nail clipper he fashioned a hook from his safety pin, and I sharpened it with a fingernail file. I found a worm under a stump, and tying the line to the umbrella, crept up to the stream.

This was a pretty far-fetched situation, I thought to myself— fishing with makeshift gear—and fishing in dead earnest, not for sport. I recalled one of my father's statements, "Always at hand is the thing needed, if you only have the wit and wisdom to recognize it." Was this wit and wisdom, I asked myself, or inspiration?

I dangled the line over the grassy bank and floated it downstream.

Can this be the way the Lord is going to answer our prayer, I thought, or do I just have a flair for the unusual? Well, we're his servants. We're promised that the way will be opened. The Lord had answered us before. Now why can't he arrange to have that fish bite? He's brought us this far, and—WHAM!

I pulled, fast! The trout sailed over my head, off the hook, and onto the bank.

"Man!" I chortled, "Mr. Fish musta been pretty hungry too."

Elder B. was laughing. But there were tears in his eyes. I stared incredulously, first at the umbrella, then at the fish. Elder B. broke the spell.

"Find another worm," he said. "There must be more fish in that brook."

Worms there were, and trout too. They hit that line as if they hadn't seen a fly or worm in weeks. It didn't take me long to catch five more. It was too good to be true. In a few short minutes six trout were broiling over a fire.

We didn't eat those fish without blessing them. And when we said, "Father in heaven, we thank thee for this food," it came from the heart. We ate them, relished them, fins and all. We were warm inside when we finished—warm from the fish, warm from deep-rooted gratitude.

We picked up our suitcases and began trudging down the narrow road.

"You know," said Elder B., as we walked with renewed strength, "the Lord is a mighty generous employer!" (*Improvement Era*, March, 1948, p. 15.)

All you need to pray is a willing heart and a particle of faith. Never be afraid to pray. Men and boys reach their greatest stature when they kneel to pray. Daily prayer will help you live worthy of the Aaronic Priesthood, and it will prepare you for life. Remember that nothing is too hard for the Lord. He can help you when all others fail. And he is always available.

Chapter 6

Blessings of Work in the Priesthood

M any years ago, as a young husband and father, I worked for a grocery chain. My shift was from about 5:30 A.M. to 2:00 P.M., without a lunch hour. I preferred it that way. Once a week I got a day off. The stake president had announced a need for brethren to work on our stake farm. We were to get the bales of hay out of the fields before it rained.

I volunteered to go out on my day off. A member of the stake presidency, Francis Bromley, took me out to the farm. Much of the hay had been baled the preceding Saturday. I suggested to President Bromley that he could drive the tractor. I would load the hay on the skids, then transfer it to the flatbed truck, and then haul it to a location where it was to be stacked. It was a hot summer day. There seemed to be no breeze at all—no shade or cloud cover. I was accustomed to hard work, but not in the sun. For hours we worked together, retrieving the baled hay from the fields. I can recall to this day how tired I was. Hay dust and dirt filled my nostrils and was caked on my arms and face. Sweat poured from my body. My hands grew numb and my arms and legs were tired, but we worked on until the work was done. I remember the feelings I had at the end of the day. President Bromley somehow knew that I had worked with all my energy to save him as much work as possible. He was not a young man, and the work was heavy. He was very kind in his appraisal of the work we had done.

The greater reward came to me on the way home. I realized that I had worked for the Lord about as hard as I knew how to work. My sinuses burned from the dust and dirt. My eyes were filled with hay dust. Perspiration and alfalfa clung to my skin and clothes. I was exhausted and probably dehydrated. My head throbbed and my muscles ached, but deep inside I had a feeling of pride. For a few moments at the end of that day, I drank from the living waters of Christ. I felt the cooling breeze of service, and I felt the shade of contentment to my soul. I have never forgotten how I felt about President Bromley. Serving him and trying to do extra work to protect him filled my soul with a deep love for him. I knew that he could see into my heart and that he knew what I was trying to do for him. I think he loved me also. I believe, however, that the greater love will come to those who serve someone else. If you want to love someone, serve that person. Service is work. It takes effort.

It has always been easy for me to accept work assignments. I have never resented them or felt imposed upon, no matter how often I was asked. Somehow God built into my spirit a feeling that it is a privilege to do anything in the kingdom. It is not a sacrifice; it has always been a blessing.

The Aaronic Priesthood in our ward often went to Welfare Square to help can, label, or do other work. Generally we were given a little slip of paper that told how many hours we had labored. To this day there is a special pride in my heart as I think back on these times. I have only slips of paper with a few handwritten figures on them, but they represent time I spent on the Lord's errand.

As an elder in Boise, one evening I was working on the stake farm with Brother Merlin Olsen from our bishopric.

As I recall, only the two of us were there. One of our jobs was to repair some power lines. Ever since my childhood I have feared electricity. Even now I turn off all the power in the house if I am going to repair some electrical equipment.

Merlin was going to go up the power pole but, although I feared what had to be done, I was younger and knew that I must do it. I asked him what to do. He gave me clear and complete instructions. I was to climb up the pole, take one wire, strip off the insulation about six inches, then take the other wire and strip off the insulation about six inches, join the wires together and then reinsulate them.

I asked him if the power was off. He assured me that it was. I climbed the pole and followed his instructions. No one will know how difficult it was for me to take that large, high-powered line in my hand, strip off the insulation, then hold that wire and the connecting wire in my hand, splice them together, and reinsulate them. Merlin was right. There was no power in the lines. I was absolutely safe.

The thing that I remember about that experience is that I had some doubt about whether the power was off or not. I was afraid that someone else on the farm might throw the breaker and turn on the electricity. Nevertheless, my faith in Merlin and the fact that I was doing what the Lord wanted me to was enough to overcome my fear.

I have always loved working in the Church. It joins us with some of the finest people on earth. Work is a discipline. It takes energy, commitment, and time. Work is necessary for repentance. Sweat and effort under the right conditions purge and cleanse the soul.

During my first assignment in Boise, I was called to serve as the priests quorum adviser. There were twenty-three priests in the old Boise Ninth Ward. Two were serving in the military. Nineteen of the twenty-one received individual awards. The bishop of the ward was Floyd Fletcher. What a bishop! What a Scouter! Every year the ward provided welfare to the storehouse through the beans we raised, picked, and canned.

When the beans were ready for harvest, the whole ward went to work.

We picked the beans early in the morning before going to work. The bean patch buzzed with brethren and sisters working up and down the rows. Working alongside my priests was a joy I shall never forget. Even though it was early in the morning and fairly cool, we would soon work up a sweat. We would talk about swimming in the cold mountain rivers where we had our annual Aaronic Priesthood outings. We shared personal stories, laughed and joked, and had a great time. This work was not a burden; it was fun. No one resented being asked to work. In fact, I think people would have felt left out if they hadn't been involved.

I remember one morning, about 7:30, when we were finishing up so we could get back home to get ready to go to work. One of the priests challenged all the others and me to take a swim in the canal. In only a moment, a priests quorum adviser and all the priests were swimming. At that early hour the cold water took our breath away. I can still feel the love and fellowship I had with that quorum of priests.

I remember one of our Aaronic Priesthood campouts during the summer. (I believe we camped on the North Fork of the Payette River.) One night, after our traditional campfire, we went swimming in the river. It was a clear night. The moon was overhead. We had a special swimming hole in the river where we swam during the day. We would dive off a rock into a deep hole, and then the current would sweep us downstream thirty or forty yards. It was great. We swam for about half an hour. Then we got dressed, and somewhere near midnight all of my priests and I locked arms and walked back down the road to camp singing "Redeemer of Israel." To this day, almost every time I sing that hymn I have a reflection in my mind from years past of a group of Aaronic Priesthood boys and their leader walking down a dirt road, under a full moon, singing together.

The work of the Aaronic Priesthood is necessary. Work is service and service is work. We need all kinds of activities in the Aaronic Priesthood, including athletics, Scouting, dances, and parties, but these must be blended with work if a quorum is to function the way it should. Work brings about a blending of spirits, a compatibility among quorum members, a trust and reliance on each other. And it brings a spirit of brotherhood that comes only to those who pay the price to have it.

You are assigned by your bishopric to perform some services and work. You need to faithfully fulfill every assignment. But there is another work that no one may see and that may seem to carry no reward. That is the work you do in a quiet way around your home without being told. It includes keeping your room clean, taking pride in it, and watching for opportunities to do work that will relieve the pressure on your parents—mowing the lawn, weeding the garden, shoveling the walks in the winter, putting out the garbage, doing the dishes, and vacuuming the house.

My young friend, you actually have to experience the internal rewards and feelings that come when you do things on your own rather than being told. This work will give you a feeling of maturity—a "magnificent obsession," Lloyd Douglas called it. It brings rewards far beyond what doing the same work brings after your parents tell you to do it.

When I was about ten or eleven, most of our relatives from the Stockton area came to visit. There must have been thirty-five or forty. Mother had invited them all to dinner. After dinner, everyone went into the living room and sat down to visit. There were piles of dirty dishes and silverware everywhere. The food had not been put away, and there were dirty pots and pans from all the cooking.

I remember thinking that later on everyone would leave and my mother would have all the cleaning up to do. An idea struck me. I started cleaning up. It was in the days before electric dishwashers. Mother had always been very clean, and she had taught us how to wash and wipe dishes correctly. I started in on this mountain of work. Finally, about three hours later, I had finished drying the last dish. I had put away all the food, cleaned off all the counters, and cleaned the sinks and the floor. The kitchen was spotless.

I will never forget the look on Mom's face later that night when all the guests had left and she came into the kitchen to clean up. I was wet from my chest to my knees. It was worth every particle of effort I had made just to see the look on Mom's face. It was a mixture of joy, relief, and pride. I made a decision then that I would try to put that look back on her face over and over again. I think I was able to do that.

Now no one should suppose that I did everything right. I could have been a lot better. But I think Mom would agree that I honestly tried.

Work in your home. Work with the members of your quorum. Work by assignment from the bishop. But work! Work is essential to your maturity. People may grow up physically, but without learning to work they are never fully mature. The work of the priesthood is no more nor less than service to God, for "when ye are in the service of your fellow beings [your quorum members, mom, dad, brother, sister, or neighbor] ye are only in the service of your God." (Mosiah 2:17.)

Chapter 7

Friends in the
Aaronic Priesthood

I believe that you and your friends in the Aaronic Priesthood are like a marching army of God. This thought inspired me to write the following poem:

The clarion call is sounding from the temple towers to hill,
  And youth today are assembling, and others coming still.
They come in bands of ten, and hundreds more approach.
  They respond to any leader, adviser, friend, or coach.
They have within their hearts deep whisperings from the past,
  For a generation of our youth, who'll be one of the last
to walk upon the earth, before the Master's time,
  When he will culminate his work, and make all lives sublime.
But that time is not yet, and the clarion call is clear,
  For the evil one has ever raged, with lust and godless fear.
He has amassed the greatest evil ever thrust upon our youth.
  His ranks are filled with evil men, disguised in shrouds of truth.

Satanic are his ways, and his workers number legion.
  He sets his hand in every land, in village, town, and region.
He walks in darkness all his days; in him no light is found.
  He hopes to shackle every youth and silence the clarion sound.

Come join our ranks, oh youth, and stand on Zion's hill,
   As fair as the sun and moon and stars; let not your voice be
still,
For the foe advances fearfully, his banners yet more terrible—
   Enslave the mind, break down the will, continuing on,
unbearable.
So, youth of light, prepare for the battle, rise up in royal bands.
   March 'gainst the foe and wield the sword, defend with heart
and hands.
This is the day, for come what may, we will win against the
foe.
   Day's end is near, the signal's clear, death cometh soon or
slow.

Advance ye hosts of God, and lift your torches high.
   The flame of truth burns in our hearts, the victory is nigh.
And yet the battle's fiercest test lies in the valley just ahead,
   For we march under glorious banners, and face the task with
dread.
We'll march into the millennium with our banners raised in
glory.
   For hosts and legions of our God will repeat the oft-told
story
Of the latter generation who fought with such great might
   And won the victory, though laboring, throughout the long,
long night.
How glorious is the army of the children of our God
   Who arm themselves in righteousness and walk the paths he
trod.

My life has been blessed by my friends, my fellow war-
riors in God's army, in the Aaronic Priesthood, the M.I.A.,
Scouting, athletics, and cultural activities in the Church.

Years ago, a boy named Dene Kesler was the deacons
quorum president in my ward. Dene was a very special young
man. One morning during priesthood meeting, he visited our
elders quorum. He presented to us some money that his
quorum had raised for the ward building fund. I served as

Scoutmaster in that ward for a short time, and I came to know the heart of my wonderful young friend. We went golfing together at 4:30 in the morning. Dene always picked me up. More than once before it was light, I have driven a golf ball out into the darkness, unable to see it after it left the tee. It seems that Dene always found his ball, but I seldom did. We had an unusual friendship over the years. We floated several major rivers together. We sat by campfires and told stories, took nightly swims, and shared almost every kind of outdoor experience together. Dene was called to go on a mission. He served in Great Britain under President Marion D. Hanks. I spoke at Dene's farewell. Dene was an outstanding missionary. Sometime during his mission he wrote me a letter. He said some kind words and then included this poem. And, after all these years, I would like to quote it back to Dene Kesler, my great young friend, and to you:

There's a comforting thought at the close of the day,
When I'm weary and lonely and sad,
That sort of grips hold of my crusty old heart
And bids it be merry and glad.
It gets in my soul and it drives out the blues,
And finally thrills through and through.
It is just a sweet memory that chants the refrain:
"I'm glad I touched shoulders with you!"

Did you know you were brave, did you know you were strong?
Did you know there was one leaning hard?
Did you know that I waited and listened and prayed,
And was cheered by your simplest word?
Did you know that I longed for the smile on your face,
For the sound of your voice ringing true?
Did you know that I grew stronger and better because
I had merely touched shoulders with you?

I am glad that I live, that I battle and strive
For the place that I know I must fill;
I am thankful for sorrows, I'll meet with a grin
What fortunes may send, good or ill.
I may not have wealth, I may not be great,

But I know I shall always be true,
For I have in my life that courage you gave
When once I rubbed shoulders with you.

(In Hazel Felleman, comp., *The Best Loved Poems of the American People*
[Garden City, New York: Garden City Publishing Co., 1936], p. 126.)

I thank Dene for sharing this great poem with me. I have
quoted it to my wife, my missionaries, my counselors in
priesthood callings, Church general boards, and prophets of
the living God. I am glad, Dene Kesler, that I touched shoulders with you.

In 1956 I was transfered to Boise, Idaho. Along with
myriads of choice friends, I met the Dennis Flake family; the
oldest son, Dennis, was in my priests quorum during the
time I served as adviser. Patriarch Flake and his wife both
served missions, as did all their sons. They are a wonderful
family of chaplains, religion teachers, and church education
supervisors. What a contribution this family has made to the
Church! Dennis and Lawrence, the two older boys, have served
as mission presidents. The other sons are equally worthy.

I remember pitching silage with Dennis all day long. I
thought that I would die, but I could not stop as long as
Dennis continued. Dennis's farming background gave him a
strength of character, a purity of heart, and a love of good
and honorable men. We had many wonderful experiences
while I lived in Boise. After I moved back to Salt Lake City,
Dennis was called on a mission, and I was invited to speak
at his farewell. He went to Australia and served under Elder
Bruce R. McConkie. We wrote to each other occasionally,
and in one of the letters from Dennis was this poem by
Douglas Malloch, which I hope will inspire you as it has me:

The tree that never had to fight
For sun and sky and air and light,
That stood out in the open plain
And always got its share of rain,

Never became a forest king,
But lived and died a scrubby thing.

The man who never had to toil
To heaven from the common soil
Who never had to win his share
Of sun and sky and light and air,
Never became a manly man,
But lived and died as he began.

Good timber does not grow in ease;
The stronger wind, the tougher trees;
The farther sky, the greater length;
The more the storm, the more the strength;
By sun and cold, by rain and snows,
In tree or man, good timber grows.

Where thickest stands the forest growth
We find the patriarchs of both;
And they hold converse with the stars
Whose broken branches show the scars
Of many winds and of much strife
This is the common law of life.

(In Al Bryant, comp., *Sourcebook of Poetry* [Grand Rapids:
Zondervan Publishing House, 1968], p. 456.)

Years ago I lived in a large ward with a great number of
youth. I served as the Scoutmaster when there were fifty-
three Scouts in the troop. One young man in the ward was a
little older than the others. He had never been a Scout. His
name was Neil Schmitt. We worked in a produce department
in a grocery store that had eight full-time and six part-time
employees. We were able to help Neil become active in the
Church. When he became active, he was truly converted.
Before I got to know him, I remember seeing him once down-
town on a Saturday night, about midnight, selling news-
papers. I was impressed with his ambition. We used to discuss scriptures at work. Once we hiked to the peak of Mt.
Olympus together.

The Stansbury Park community is located west of Salt
Lake City. In that park was an ideal swimming hole, a young

man's dream. It was an old mill pond down in a gully. On the rear side was a six-foot bank that went straight down to the water. The pond was filled from an underground spring. On the bank was a large tree that leaned out over the pond. The pond was deep, and someone had nailed a board for a diving platform about six feet up the tree. This was about twelve feet above the water. There was another diving place about eighteen feet up. Then, about ten feet above that, was a large branch on which a long rope had been tied so you could swing out over the pond. Also, you could dive in from that height. You could take the rope, run down the bank, and swing in a giant circle out over the pond. Then you could drop into the pond or swing on around and crash into the tree. It was a great place.

I remember my first experience at the millpond. I challenged Neil that I would be first in the water. We walked down to the pond and changed into our swimming suits. Then Neil hesitated and I dove in. The next time we went, I gave the same challenge. He ran down (he was a sprinter) and changed into his swimming suit. I also ran but was quite a few steps behind him. Therefore he had a head start. Just as Neil was pulling on his swimming suit, I dove into the water partially undressed and beat him. The third time, Neil was determined that he would be first in the water. We had challenged each other. This time I knew that Neil meant business. He sprinted ahead of me down to the millpond. I believe he was wearing his swimming suit under his clothes. By the time I arrived at the pond, Neil was almost ready to dive in. I kicked off my shoes and dove in fully clothed. I beat him. When you are older and not so fast, you have to think of shortcuts. All through the years, we have had that kind of fun together. I really love Neil. Over the years, he has been more than a friend.

I have a friend named Jay who was in my Sunday School class years ago. We have kept in touch over the years. Along with the rest of our class, we hiked to the peak of Mt. Timpanogos in Utah Valley. We went swimming together. I attended football and basketball games in which he played. I was with him when he did some amazing things in track. He was a competitor to the core. He was a high-school student-body president. He served a great mission in France, returned home, went to medical school, and now is an orthopedic surgeon.

A few years ago I was invited as a member of the Young Men General Presidency to attend a regional youth conference in the East. When I got off the plane, there was Jay and his wife to meet me. We were both filled with emotion. I wept. He wept. His father had passed away some time before, and I gave this sweet young friend a fatherly hug. We spent two days together. Now the years have passed and Jay has been a great blessing in the life of my son Lawrence. Although we do not spend much time together, I love him dearly and am grateful for his interest and love. Jay is now serving in a mission presidency. Jay Hassell, I want you to know you have been a great influence in my life.

Now these young men have always been faithful. I know that they have had faith in Christ all their lives. Good and faithful young men need leaders who care. I want you to know that I love you—that I am just terribly proud of you. Thank you for your activity. Thanks for being consistent. Thanks for your participation and for holding fast to the iron rod. The active and faithful also need good friends with strong faithful testimonies. We need the Church and we need the activities and programs that hold us close to good leaders and strong friends that strengthen our testimonies through critical years of temptation.

God bless you for your righteousness. I am grateful that you have a believing heart, like my four young associates over the years. It means a great deal to me that you are not rebellious. Like the prodigal son's brother, you are tending to your duty. I love you, and I am humbled by your good ness. I know that you are sometimes tempted and that it is not easy to maintain your purity, but you are doing the right thing. It is easier to walk through the tempestuous years of youth if you are active in the Church and associate with good people like Dene, Dennis, Neil, and Jay, and hundreds more. It is good to spend fun times swimming, floating rivers, hiking to mountain peaks, participating in seminary and in ward dances and parties, and doing all the other wonderful things we do as members of the Church.

The service projects we do together bring joyous memories. No other service activity compares to helping someone remain active in the Church, or to activating or converting someone presently not involved. Also, I know the Lord is pleased when we care for the poor, the widow, the orphan, the homely, the lonely, the beautiful, the wealthy, the dull, the bright—all of God's children.

You have a sacred responsibility to reach out and bring to others the glorious blessings, the fun, and the excitement of this wonderful church. Hardly a good mother or father goes to bed at night without a prayer deep in their hearts for a wayward son or daughter. They grieve deeply for them. These young people need your help.

This poem shares the tender feelings of a loving mother for her wayward son:

> Where is my wandering boy tonight?
>   The boy of my tend'rest care:
> The boy that was once my joy and light,
>   The child of my love and prayer.
>
> Once he was pure as the morning dew,
>   As he knelt at his mother's knee;
> No face was so bright, no heart more true,
>   And none was as sweet as he.
>
> Oh, could I see him now, my boy,
>   As fair as in olden time,
> When prattle and smile made home a joy,
>   And life was a merry chime.
>
> Go, for my wandering boy tonight,
>   Go search for him where you will:

> But bring him to me with all his blight,
>   And tell him I love him still.
>
> *Chorus*
> Oh, where is my boy tonight?
>   where is my boy tonight?
> My heart o'erflows, for I love him, he knows,
> Oh, where is my boy tonight?
>
> (In *A Treasury of the Familiar*, edited by Ralph L. Woods
> [New York: 1978], p. 465.)

In 1985, United States vice-president George Bush shared this inspiring story at the national meeting of the Boy Scouts of America:

> Way back in 401 B.C., a young Persian prince named Cyrus hired an army of 10,000 Greek soldiers to help him take the Persian throne away from his brother. Cyrus and his Greek companions marched 1500 miles overland from the western edge of Turkey, through the deserts of Syria, and onto the plains of Iraq. They met the Persian king and the army near what is now Baghdad. The Greeks won the battle, but they lost the war when Cyrus was killed in the day's action, and that left the Greeks and their army in a terrible fix. They no longer had any cause to proceed further; they couldn't retreat eastward, for no food remained on the land, and to the north, mountains, which we know today as the wilds of Cartistan, and the highlands of Georgia and Armenia were all inhabited by savage mountain tribes. And to make things worse, the Greek commanding general and his entire staff of officers had gone to a conference with the Persians under safe conduct, and they had been assassinated. And that seemed to leave absolutely no alternative to the Greeks but to surrender and throw themselves on the mercy of the Persians. Some of you will remember this. One of the Greeks, a private in the ranks named Zenefon, had a different idea, and he voiced it to his Greek comrades: Notice that our enemies lacked the courage to fight us until they seized our general. They think that we are defeated because our officers are dead, but we'll show them that they turned us all into generals. Instead of one general, they'll have

10,000 generals against them. The Greeks spirits rallied and they resolved to fight their way through the mountains. Zenefon turned out to be a brilliant strategist and his army of 10,000 generals did reach safety, 2500 miles and four months later. Perhaps the most celebrated march of that time, celebrated escape, if you will, in western history.

We need the young men of the Aaronic Priesthood to be valiant leaders in the Lord's army. You are one of them. You must not fail—too much is at stake. May God bless you as you help yourself and your friends to serve the Lord.

Chapter 8

Crossing the Bridges of Life

I like Will Allen Dromgoole's poem "The Bridge Builder" because it reminds me of our responsibility to help others overcome the obstacles of life:

An old man traveling a lone highway,
Came at the evening cold and gray,
To a chasm vast, deep and wide,
Through which was flowing a sullen tide.
The old man crossed in the twilight dim,
The sullen stream held no fears for him;
But he turned when safe on the other side,
And builded a bridge to span the tide.
"Old man," cried a fellow pilgrim near,
"You're wasting your time in building here.
Your journey will end with the closing day;
You never again will pass this way.
You have crossed the chasm deep and wide,
Why build you this bridge at eventide?"
The builder lifted his old gray head,
"Good friend, in the path I have come," he said,
"There followeth after me today
A youth whose feet must pass this way.

> This stream, which has been as naught to me,
> To that fair-haired youth may pitfall be.
> He, too, must cross in the twilight dim,
> Good friend, I am building this bridge for him."

(In *Vital Speeches of the Day*, July 1, 1986, p. 556.)

We do have bridge builders to keep us on the right track. And, in a sense, we will mature and become bridge builders to a future generation. It was nearly 6,000 years ago when our first parents, Adam and Eve, had a son, Cain, who asked, "Am I my brother's keeper?" This question has rung down through the centuries, and always the answer of faithful members of the Lord's true kingdom is a resounding yes.

Your life is not your own to waste and squander any way you want. You have been called as a holy servant of God. Your ordination to the Aaronic Priesthood is a blessing beyond comprehension. Your life is one of commitment to the greatest cause ever espoused by president, leader, or General Authority. The gospel of Jesus Christ and its precepts will be the most important work in the eternities. You have been enlisted in it at a youthful age, and that will be a great advantage to you.

We hear about athletes, performers, and business executives who draw tremendous salaries and have great power. But when you compare the glory of these things to the glories of the gospel of Jesus Christ, they are like a flickering candle before the blazing sun. The Lord wants us to succeed in our righteous temporal goals, but we must never let these become our main objective. No other work can begin to compare with the marvelous work of the kingdom. Remember that you were born to serve others.

As a bridge builder you will be expected to assist other young men who are active or less active. This includes, when necessary, a rescue mission. When a young man in your quorum or ward begins to wander away from spiritual things, you will need to take a special interest in him and become a true friend to him. Remember that you must never compromise your standards when helping someone else in the quorum. But you can be a good example and help change the direction or the thinking of a fellow quorum member.

A truly committed deacon, teacher, or priest could never sit by while a fellow quorum member went astray. There are several things you as a bridge builder can do to help save your friends:

1. If your friends are telling dirty stories, try to change the subject by talking about something else of greater interest. If this does not work, then tell about something exciting your quorum or Scout troop is going to do or has done. Generally when you start talking about Church activities, the other subject will seem out of place.

2. Swearing, especially taking the Lord's name in vain, is offensive. Try getting your friends to substitute good words or even funny words for profanity. This will not seem preachy but fun.

3. If you are confronted with dirty magazines or books, just take a stand and say, "I will not look at or read such things." Then you can add, "Let's not read it—think what our bishop or parents would feel like if they knew we had."

4. The Word of Wisdom is important. The Lord has promised health, strength, and spiritual blessings to those who keep it. If someone wants you to break it, the only answer you can give is an absolute "No, thanks." It may sound harsh, but if you are firm, your friends will respect you for it.

5. Cheating in school or anywhere else is not worthy of you. You hold the Holy Aaronic Priesthood, and you can be guided by the Holy Ghost if you are worthy. If someone in your quorum cheats, you might ask your quorum president or adviser to give a lesson on honesty.

6. Vandalism is inspired by Satan. He makes it sound exciting to throw eggs at someone's house or car, to blow up mail boxes, or to deface property. Some years back, three young men went to a convenience store and bought several dozen eggs with a payroll check that belonged to one of the

boys. They drove a few blocks away and then threw the eggs at a large two-story home. The man who owned the home phoned the police, who checked at a few stores nearby. The clerk at the convenience store remembered the boys who had bought the eggs. In fact, she still had the check with the boy's name on it. The police picked up the boys and took them to the police station. The homeowner was there. He was a fine man who was crippled and made his way around in a wheel chair. He had done so much to help young people, such as speaking at assemblies, visiting the hospital, counseling youth who had been crippled in accidents, and so on. He was deeply hurt to think that someone would vandalize his house. One of the young men later said, "We didn't think about who was in the house or about how much it might hurt someone's feelings. We just thought about how funny it was to throw eggs." Those young men learned a great lesson. When you are with boys who talk about vandalism as if it were just a joke, consider the effect it will have on other people. Try to get your friends to do something else as a way to have fun.

7. Make every attempt to include everyone in your activities. The quorum is not meant to leave anyone out. Include every young man in every possible meeting or activity. You can never tell how important that may be. It has always been easy for me to include those who feel shy, awkward, inferior, homely, or sad as my friends. I felt the same way as I grew up. I suppose I was not sad, as I have always had a somewhat buoyant spirit; but I had many other similar problems. Make friends with and be kind to those who do not have many friends, and you will become a bridge builder like the Master.

8. Do not be a burden to your parents. Instead, be a blessing to them. You can do so much at home to make it a place of joy and happiness. Helping in the home makes everyone's load lighter. Also, you ought to earn any money you get from your parents. You ought to keep your room clean,

do your share of the chores, and then do a little extra to relieve the workload of your mother or other family members.

9. Fill with pride every duty assigned by your quorum president. Don't ever feel that doing Church work is a burden. One of the most difficult assignments I ever had was public speaking. I decided I would overcome that fear. At first every speaking assignment was a burden. Then it became a great blessing. I had to study to prepare talks. I memorized poetry and scripture, and I learned how to organize my thoughts. Now it is exciting to share the concepts, stories, principles, and poetry that I love. Filling assignments with pride and excitement builds bridges to the person you will become.

10. Always work toward a mission and temple marriage. To do that, you must stay morally clean, active in the Church, and free from drugs, alcohol, and tobacco. The Lord once said to one of his missionaries, "Lift up your heart and rejoice, for the hour of your mission is come." (D&C 31:3.) A mission is something to rejoice about and to look forward to, as is a temple marriage. Your life of active priesthood service will build a bridge that will take you to these things and eventually to the celestial kingdom.

Chapter 9

"Thou Art an Eagle"

Once a farmer took his young son on a hike. They tramped through the meadows and woods. They hiked through the pines and up over the hills. They climbed the steep mountains and finally, high above the timber line, scaled the crags and peaks. There they saw a giant eagle soaring overhead. They scanned the cliffs and finally located the nest. The boy climbed precariously up the cliff to where the nest was located. He reached into the nest, which rested on a ledge, and pulled out an egg, which he put inside his shirt. Then he climbed carefully back down the cliff.

He and his father returned home, and the boy put the egg in a nest where a hen was brooding over her eggs. By and by, when the eggs were hatched, each delivered a small chick except the one from which a young eaglet was hatched. Months passed and the eaglet matured. After the eagle was full grown, a naturalist was driving down the highway out in the country. As he drove by the farmer's yard, he saw the giant eagle. He slammed on his brakes, got out of the car, and went over to the fence. He could hardly believe his eyes. He opened the gate, walked into the yard, and found the farmer. "Where did you get that eagle?" he asked. The farmer said, "It's a chicken." The man responded: "I am a naturalist. I know all about these things, and I tell you that is an eagle. Furthermore, I'll prove it." He picked up the eagle, put it on his arm, and said, "Thou art an eagle—fly." The eagle hopped off his arm and began to scratch in the dirt like the chickens. The farmer said, "I told you it was only a chicken." The naturalist asked for a ladder. He leaned it against the barn. Then he carried the eagle up on top of the barn. He stood at the peak of the roof on the barn, placed the eagle on his arm, and said, "Thou art an eagle—fly." The eagle swooped down into the yard below and began scratching in the gravel. The farmer hollered up, "I told you it was a chicken."

The man climbed down off the barn. He made an agreement with the farmer. The next morning, long before sunrise, he picked up the eagle. He carried it through the woods and over the meadows. He continued up into the hills and the pines, onward, upward, above the timberline to the peaks and crags and pinnacles of the mountains. He arrived at the mountaintop just before dawn. As the first rays of the sun began to streak across the sky, he put the eagle on his arm. The fresh, cool winds came through the valleys and trees below and swept up to the cliff where the naturalist stood. The eagle breathed deeply. The first streaks of sunlight caught his eye. He stretched his giant wings, almost six feet across. The naturalist said, "Thou art an eagle—fly." The eagle slowly lifted off the naturalist's arm. It ascended into the sky. It soared higher and higher and further and further. It saw more in an instant than its companions had in an entire lifetime, and from that time forth it was never again content to be a barnyard fowl.

Once you have felt the power and exhilaration of truly magnifying your priesthood, you will no longer be content to be an ordinary young man. You will want to represent God on the earth and to be one of his holy and choice servants.

Some of your Aaronic Priesthood duties may include passing the sacrament, gathering fast offerings, delivering messages for the bishop and his counselors, and home teaching. But you also have other responsibilities that are a little more subtle but still vitally important.

Dressing appropriately. Be sure that you look like a servant of the Lord as you perform your duties. When passing the sacrament, wear a dress shirt and tie. Avoid loud or gaudy clothing that would attract the attention of others and take their minds off the sacrament. Make sure your hair is neat and short enough that it does not give you a feminine appearance or distract people's concentration.

For some people, you will be their only contact with the Church, so you need to represent the Church well. For example, you will gather fast offerings from some people who never go to church. And your brief visit can have a powerful influence on them if you look and act as you should. Your appearance should be neat and clean. Your conduct should be dignified and yet warm and friendly. A home-teaching assignment ought to be carried out in the same dignified manner. And you should always be prepared to bear your testimony to a family if your senior companion invites you to.

Behaving properly. As an Aaronic Priesthood holder, you should conduct yourself properly in all things. This is especially true at the sacrament table. You have probably seen immature deacons who are not as reverent as they should be. These young men should be taught that they are violating the sacred trust the Lord has given them to help with the sacrament. The teachers and priests should set a proper example to those who are younger. We do not have a double standard in the Church; all should refrain from telling dirty stories, reading pornographic magazines, using profane language, or being abusive or rude. It takes maturity to live gospel standards, and those young men who do will find success in the world and great opportunities for service in God's kingdom.

Staying worthy. All of your priesthood assignments should be determined by your worthiness. You should be honest in all your dealings. You should always tell the truth. Never should you lie or cheat at home, at school, or at a place of entertainment. Be morally clean and pure in thought. Never violate the Word of Wisdom or be involved in drugs. Your concern should be to prove yourself worthy every day of your life. As you do, growth, development, and success will be yours. One of the greatest goals you can have is to become pure in heart. As you faithfully strive to live worthy, you will achieve this goal.

Once you have served with love, devotion, commitment and dignity, you will never again be content to do less. You will be like the eagle. An eagle represents leadership, strength, and greatness. It represents power and should be a constant reminder of your priesthood power. Becoming an Eagle Scout, too, is a high achievement for a young man. It represents the finest and noblest in us. Achieving it is worth the effort. Those who soar high will see much, do much, and be rewarded greatly.

Part 3

Examples to Live By

Chapter 10

Great Examples from the Book of Mormon

The Book of Mormon is another witness of Christ. Joseph Smith called it "the most correct of any book on the earth, and the keystone of our religion." He also said that we could get nearer to God by following its teachings than we could by following the teachings of any other book. (*History of the Church* 4:461.)

The Book of Mormon holds special significance for holders of the Aaronic Priesthood, which is a preparatory priesthood. No preparation in the Church is complete without reading and studying the Book of Mormon. A testimony of the Book of Mormon will come as you open its pages and read.

You have a right to know of the truthfulness of the book. If the book is true, then Joseph Smith was a true prophet of the living God. If it is not true, then he was a fraud. You must read for yourself the sacred words written by the holy prophets of the Book of Mormon to gain a personal testimony.

As a young man, I read the Book of Mormon. You do not have to be an "intellectual" or to have a sophisticated knowledge of scriptural language, nor do you have to understand all that you read in order to learn from the Book of Mormon. There is a spirit in the Book of Mormon that pervades every page. You will feel it as you read it. You will almost hear the voices of the prophets who have recorded sacred words of testimony. Wisdom will come to you from its pages. If you read with a sincere heart, with real intent to know of its truthfulness, having faith in Christ, the Holy Ghost will show you that it is true.

The Lord Jesus Christ, in a solemn oath that will ring across the eternities, declared, "[Joseph Smith] has translated the Book, even that part which I have commanded him, *and as your Lord and your God liveth it is true.*" (D&C 17:6; italics added.)

One day every soul who will read the Book of Mormon as prescribed by Moroni will have that same witness. I know that as my Lord and God lives it is true. I can actually feel the power in his words, and you can too. The Spirit will carry his words to your heart.

I have often said that I would rather lose my life than have the influence of the Book of Mormon taken from my life. I have a love for the prophets of the Book of Mormon that is beyond the power of words to describe. I have often thought how empty my life would be if the knowledge, experience, and feelings I have received through that book were suddenly removed from my soul.

Imagine what it would be like not to know Nephi or his father Lehi. What if we had never heard the words of King Benjamin, or never read of the ministries of Alma and his son? What if we were unacquainted with Ammon or his brethren? Can you imagine the loss to patriotism if we had never heard of Captain Moroni and his "title of liberty"?

Consider the loss to a dark and confused world if we had no record of Jesus visiting "his other sheep" who were on this continent. What a loss if we knew not Mahonri Moriancumr (the brother of Jared) or General Mormon and his beloved son Moroni.

The Book of Mormon is magnificent. In dozens and dozens of readings I have come to love it with every particle of my soul. It contains many things that will impress you and bear witness to your soul that the book is true. Read a few pages each morning or night. Study and underline the things that impress you. Make notes in the margins of the things you want to remember. Make it your book.

As you read, you will come to love the mighty prophet Nephi, who was large in stature. You will appreciate his loyalty to his father, Lehi. You will find a faith in Nephi that will charge your soul with power.

You will travel with Nephi in vision with the Spirit of the Lord. You will be privileged to see in your mind's eye the same vision Lehi received and Nephi desired. You will learn of the interpretation of the dream.

You will see the rod of iron leading to the tree of life, whose fruit is most precious above all. You will see the large and spacious building and those who mock the humble servants of God, and you will liken it unto our day.

You will travel through the vast wilderness and wastelands, and you will feel the Lord's direction to his young prophet. Nephi will build a ship as commanded by the Lord. You will hear his older brothers, Laman and Lemuel, criticize him and threaten to take his life. Then you will see Nephi, delivered by the Lord, stand in all his majesty and declare to his brothers: "In the name of the Almighty God, I command you that ye touch me not, for I am filled with the power of God, even unto the consuming of my flesh; and whoso shall lay his hands upon me shall wither even as a dried reed; and he shall be as naught before the power of God, for God shall smite him. . . . If God had commanded me to do all things I could do them. If he should command me that I should say unto this water, be thou earth, it should be earth; and if I should say it, it would be done." (1 Nephi 17:48-51.)

You will come to love the faithful brothers of Nephi—Sam, Jacob, and Joseph. You will read Nephi's declaration that his brother Jacob "also has seen [the Savior] as I have seen him." (2 Nephi 11:3.)

You will go hunting with Enos the son of Jacob. You will be deeply moved as this splendid young man kneels in humble prayer and prays all the day long, and when the night comes he is still on his knees. You will witness the answer to his prayer and feel the mercy of God.

King Benjamin will march onto the scene, and you will see the tower erected so that his voice might be heard. Your interest will be kindled as King Benjamin promises his people a new name by which they shall be known, a name that will never be blotted out, a name to distinguish them from all other people. (Mosiah 1:11-12.) You will thrill with the multitude as they receive their new name, "the children of Christ." (Mosiah 5:7.)

Abinadi, a holy prophet, will stand before King Noah and the king's court and call these wicked people to repentance. His words will carry such fire that the king himself will fear. Then you will be a witness to evil priests who unjustly accuse Abinadi and burn him to death. A witness will come into your heart that this courageous, holy prophet of God became a martyr for the Lord's work. You will be humbled to witness in your mind the conduct of a valiant servant of God who loves the Lord more than he loves life.

Kings will be converted and be willing give up all they possess just to know God. King Mosiah's son Ammon will work in the stables and tend the sheep of King Lamoni to gain favor in his sight. As in the days of Moses, David, and Gideon, you will see Ammon stand and contend with many men, slaying some and cutting off the arms of all who raise their swords against him.

Alma will declare, "O that I were an angel, and could have the wish of mine heart, that I might go forth and speak with the trump of God, with a voice to shake the earth, and cry repentance unto every people!" (Alma 29:1.) You will feel the tenderness and sincerity of his plea and gain a sacred feeling for your future mission when you also will declare those words.

The spiritual excitement and thrilling experiences of the prophets will pull you through the pages. Captain Moroni will be raised up by the Lord as a defender of liberty and freedom. He will be described in these words: "Moroni was a strong and mighty man; he was a man of perfect understanding; yea, a man that did not delight in bloodshed; a man whose soul did joy in the liberty and the freedom of his country, and his brethren from bondage and slavery; yea, a man whose heart did swell with thanksgiving to his God, for the many privileges and blessings which he bestowed upon his people; a man who did labor exceedingly for the welfare and safety of his people. Yea, and he was a man who was firm in the faith of Christ, and he had sworn with an oath to defend his people, his rights, and his country, and his religion, even to the loss of his blood. . . . Yea, verily, verily I say unto you, if all men had been, and were, and ever would be, like unto Moroni, behold, the very powers of hell would have been shaken forever; yea, the devil would never have power over the hearts of the children of men." (Alma 48:11-12, 17.)

The climax of your reading will come as you read the prophecies of Samuel the Lamanite. Then you will witness in your mind's eye the most terrible destruction ever to come upon the inhabitants of the earth. There will be smoke and fire and earthquakes. High places will be made low, and low places will be lifted up. Mountains will be cast down. Rivers will be turned loose. The seas will cast up waves of destruction. There will be lightning and thunder, and hosts of the living will give up their lives and be sent to their eternal reward.

Thick darkness will settle over all the land. Agonizing voices of suffering people who were spared will wail into the night. Despair will prevail. Then the voice of the Redeemer will be heard across the land. If you listen carefully, you will feel the sadness and sorrow in his heart as he declares, "How oft would I have gathered you as a hen gathereth her chickens under her wings . . . and ye would not." (3 Nephi 10:5.)

Weeks later, gathered by the temple in the land Bountiful, the people will see "a Man descending out of heaven; . . . clothed in a white robe." (3 Nephi 11:8.)

You will watch the people go forth to thrust their hands into the Savior's side and feel the nail prints in his hands and feet. You will hear them cry out: "Hosanna! Blessed be the name of the Most High God!" (3 Nephi 11:17.)

Imagine the thrill of listening to the resurrected Savior! For several chapters you will read his words, as recorded by the prophets. You will be a witness when he blesses the blind, the sick, the lame, and the leprous, and heals them. You will see angels come out of heaven and minister to the little children.

Three of the twelve disciples will be chosen to tarry until he comes in his glorious second coming. You will occasionally hear testimony from those who have been ministered to by the Three Nephites.

Even with only a partial comprehension of all you read, the truth of the Book of Mormon will burn in your mind.

This is only the smallest part of what you will read. I promise you that you will gain a testimony of the divinity of the Book of Mormon and its translator, Joseph Smith. Once you know the the Book of Mormon is true, you will always know how to keep your testimony.

Enemies of the Church, some within and some without, try to disprove the doctrines of the Church. They want you to read their lies to weaken your testimony. There are evil men and women who will attempt to shake your belief. You need not fear. Every time someone tries to tear down your testimony, remember this counsel:

1. Do not read anti-Mormon literature. It is theological pornography. Enemies of the Church may argue that we are afraid of reading these evil materials. But this is not true. We do not read anti-Mormon literature because it is offensive to God.

2. Go back and read a few pages, anywhere you like, in the Book of Mormon. Ponder and pray over each page, asking God if Joseph Smith could possibly have written those words. The Lord will bear witness to your soul that "as your Lord and your God liveth" the book is true.

3. Consider our wonderful and holy prophet of God, President Ezra Taft Benson, his counselors, the Council of the Twelve, the other General Authorities, your stake president, and your bishop. These are men of integrity. They would not lie. Only the Holy Ghost can bear witness of the truth of the gospel to our spirits. Only the members of this church can bear an absolute and revealed testimony that the church is true. That is the strength of the Latter-day Saint position.

Once again, as I conclude this chapter, I tell you in truth and soberness, willing to place all that I possess on the altar, that I know that the Book of Mormon is true. I love it with every particle of my soul. As God lives, it is true! And you too can have that witness.

Chapter 11

David, King of Israel

I t was said of David that he had a heart like God's own heart. (Acts 13:22.) Could there possibly be a greater compliment to any soul that walks the earth? David's purity gave him spiritual, mental, and physical strength.

When David was chided by his brothers for leaving the sheep and coming to the battlefield where Israel was challenged by the Philistines, he said, "Is there not a cause?" (1 Samuel 17:29.) King Saul granted David permission to battle Goliath. Then the giant, seeing only a boy in a shepherd's cloak, challenged him: "Am I a dog, that thou comest to me with staves? And the Philistine cursed David by his gods. And the Philistine said to David, Come to me, and I will give thy flesh unto the fowls of the air, and to the beasts of the field." (1 Samuel 17:43-44.)

Then David, who was "but a youth . . . and of a fair countenance" (1 Samuel 17:42) responded in words that thrill the soul. He knew the source of his power: "Thou comest to me with a sword, and with a spear, and with a shield: but I come to thee in the name of the Lord of hosts, the God of the armies of Israel, whom thou has defied. This day will the Lord deliver thee into mine hand; and I will smite thee, and take thine head from thee; and I will give the carcases of the host of the Philistines this day unto the fowls of the air, and to the wild beasts of the earth; that all the earth may know that there is a God in Israel." (1 Samuel 17:45-46.)

Then what a moment for Israel as "David hasted, and ran toward the army to meet the Philistine." (1 Samuel 17:48.) A great victory took place that day. Goliath was defeated and Israel took heart. David continued to walk in the ways of God, and, as Samuel the Prophet had so anointed him, one day he became king.

We must always be careful when we walk in high places or have special privileges. If we do not maintain our purity, then we can suffer serious consequences. Francois René de Chateaubriand said, "In days of service all things are founded, in days of special privilege they deteriorate, and in days of vanity they are destroyed." Several weaknesses may have crept silently into David's life, for he became a king and a conqueror with many wives and concubines and with undisciplined appetites.

The Bible tells us that in a time when "kings go forth to battle," David stayed home and "sent Joab" instead. If he had done his duty, he would have gone to battle and possibly saved himself. But instead, he lazily stayed at home and committed a grave sin: "It came to pass in an eveningtide, that David arose from off his bed, and walked upon the roof of the king's house: and from the roof he saw a woman washing herself; and the woman was very beautiful to look upon. And David sent and enquired after the woman. And one said, Is not this Bathsheba, the daughter of Eliam, the wife of Uriah the Hittite?" (2 Samuel 11:1-3.)

It sounds as though even the servant was trying to warn David to leave this woman alone, that she had a husband— Uriah. The king in his authority overrode the servant and sent for Bathsheba. What a different story it might have been if he had gone down and run around the palace a dozen times or done 100 pushups.

Instead, "she came in unto him, and he lay with her. And the woman conceived, and sent and told David, and said, I am with child." (2 Samuel 11:4-5.)

David was sinking into deeper, more far-reaching transgression, and without repentance that is always the case. Sin is like quicksand that drags us down to death.

David sent for Uriah who was with the armies that David should have been leading. If Uriah returned home, thought David, and slept with Bathsheba, he would think the child was his, and David's sin would still be covered. David had Uriah report, and then he sent food and drink to Uriah's home. But Uriah, knowing that brave men were dying on the field of battle, would not indulge himself in desires of the flesh. He was a man of honor. This frustrated David's plan all the more, and finally David's goodness and character had deterioriated so far that he had Uriah deliver a sealed message to Joab: "Set ye Uriah in the forefront of the hottest battle, and retire ye from him, that he may be smitten, and die." (2 Samuel 11:15.)

Could this be the same David who had a heart like God's own heart? Joab must have wondered. Obediently he "assigned Uriah unto a place where he knew that valiant men were" (verse 16), and Uriah was killed.

What tragic consequences sin brings! Think for a moment of the temptations that were thrust before David. He must have found Bathsheba exciting, beautiful, and desirable. His physical desires took over the reasoning of his mind and the whisperings of the Spirit. President David O. McKay once said that no act is ever committed unless it is first justified in the mind. David lusted, desired, and fulfilled the pleasures he had imagined. There is sometimes pleasure, excitement, and even satisfaction in sinning. If this were not so, who would sin? But consequences are severe, and a day of accountability always comes.

Listen now to David's words of remorse for his few small moments of pleasure. In the 38th psalm, he describes his condition as he finally sorrows for his sins: "Thine arrows stick fast in me, and thy hand presseth me sore. There is no soundness in my flesh because of thine anger; neither is there any rest in my bones because of my sin. For mine iniquities are gone over mine head: as an heavy burden they are too heavy for me. My wounds stink and are corrupt because of my foolishness. I am troubled; I am bowed down greatly; I go mourning all the day long. For my loins are filled with a loathsome disease: and there is no soundness in my flesh. I am feeble and sore broken: I have roared by reason of the disquietness of my heart. Lord, all my desire is before thee; and my groaning is not hid from thee. My heart panteth, my strength faileth me: as for the light of mine eyes, it also is gone from me. My lovers and my friends stand aloof from my sore; and my kinsmen stand afar off. . . . But I, as a deaf man, heard not; and I was as a dumb man that openeth not his mouth. . . . For I am ready to halt, and my sorrow is continually before me. For I will declare mine iniquity; I will be sorry for my sin." (Psalm 38:2-11, 13, 17, 18.)

In some small way David's purity of heart was restored through repentance. Oh, what a blessing it would have been to David if only he had known in the beginning what he knew in the end.

What a contrast to the life of David is the life of Job. Satan, who was jealous of Job, said to the Lord: "Doth Job fear God for nought? Hast not thou made an hedge about him, and about his house, and about all that he hath on every side? Thou hast blessed the work of his hands, and his substance is increased in the land." (Job 1:9-10.)

A great truth is taught here. The Lord makes a hedge to protect us and our homes and all that we have. The hedges come from keeping the commandments and walking in God's path.

You must combat these evils with every particle of your soul. You must keep yourself clean, free, and pure. You must not be involved in sexual relations before marriage. Purity, self-restraint, and virtue are God's holy ways. You may choose to sin or not, but you cannot remove the consequences. You must either repent or suffer. The Lord has warned: "I command you to repent— repent, lest I smite you by the rod of my mouth, and by my wrath, and by my anger, and your sufferings be sore—how sore you know not, how exquisite you know not, yea, how hard to bear you know not. For behold, I, God, have suffered these things for all, that they might not suffer if they would repent; but if they would not repent they must suffer even as I; which suffering caused myself, even God, the greatest of all, to tremble because of pain, and to bleed at every pore, and to suffer both body and spirit—and would that I might not drink the bitter cup, and shrink." (D&C 19:15-18.)

David was a great soul who let weakness and temptation remove him from favor in the Lord's sight. But he humbled himself to the dust of the earth. His heart returned, as it was in the beginning, to be like God's own heart. We see this magnificent king of Israel in his later years regaining favor in the Lord's eyes. He wrote: "The Lord is my shepherd; I shall not want. He maketh me to lie down in green pastures: he leadeth me beside the still waters. He restoreth my soul: he leadeth me in the paths of righteousness for his name's sake. Yea, though I walk through the valley of the shadow of death, I will fear no evil: for thou art with me; thy rod and thy staff they comfort me. Thou preparest a table before me in the presence of mine enemies: thou anointest my head with oil; my cup runneth over. Surely goodness and mercy shall follow me all the days of my life: and I will dwell in the house of the Lord for ever." (Psalm 23.)

Chapter 12

Elijah

We read in the Bible about a man who had absolute integrity. His name was Elijah, and he was a prophet of God. He feared no man, only God. He had been sanctified through a spartan life. He had been hammered and molded as an instrument of God. The anvil against which he was hammered was unyielding, and he seemed to absorb the iron into his soul.

Elijah was sent by the Lord to the wicked King Ahab, to whom he declared, "As the Lord God of Israel liveth, before whom I stand, there shall not be dew nor rain these years, but according to my word." (1 Kings 17:1.)

Here was a holy prophet of God who probably looked more like the wilderness from which he came than a messenger of Jehovah. We wonder at Ahab's attitude and suppose that he and his servants mocked and cursed Elijah.

The Lord had this humble servant leave and hide himself "by the brook Cherith." (1 Kings 17:3.) The Lord promised Elijah that he would drink from the brook and that ravens would be sent to feed him there.

The next verse gives us insight into "the word of the Lord." (1 Kings 17:5.) Elijah did not wonder about how the Lord would keep his promises. In faith he followed the word of God. "And the ravens brought him bread and flesh in the morning, and bread and flesh in the evening; and he drank of the brook." (1 Kings 17:6.)

After a while, the brook dried up "because there had been no rain." (1 Kings 17:7.) Then "the word of the Lord came unto him, saying, Arise, get thee to Zarephath [for] . . . behold, I have commanded a widow woman there to sustain thee." (1 Kings 17:8-9.)

Elijah was not without heart. He knew conditions were hard not only for the king and his wicked prophets and servants but even more so for a widow. Again, without hesitation, he complied with the Lord's direction.

Some Church members today are absolutely committed to the Lord. They are the obedient and humble followers of Christ. They do not doubt. They do not vary their course. The winds of adversity do not sway their thinking. Popular opinions and public acclaim have no influence on them. They have charted their course and stick to it.

Such was the widow to whom Elijah was sent. The Lord told Elijah that he had commanded the woman to sustain him. And yet it appears from the scriptures that the widow was unaware of Elijah's arrival. When did the Lord command her? Could it have been after study and prayer when a conviction of the truth of Jehovah's word became a guide in her life? Could it have come to her through a life of sacrifice and obedience? I think so. Nevertheless, the command was not a specific command to sustain a holy prophet of God, as she was unaware of his needs. The command to her, as it is to all of us, is a constant command to live all of the gospel all of the time. If this experience were to happen in my life, the Lord would not need to tell me to sustain the prophet. Every act, every covenant, all that I understand shouts a command in my ears to sustain the prophets. Somehow deep in my soul I think the Lord knows I would feed his prophet even if I had to go without.

The woman was where the Lord said she would be—at the gate of the city gathering sticks. And I think Elijah, filled with emotion and knowing the suffering of this widow, may have been tried to the limit to ask her, "Fetch me, I pray thee, a little water in a vessel, that I may drink." (1 Kings 17:10.) There was no hesitation whatever on her part. She simply left what she was doing and humbly obeyed. She may or may not have known that Elijah was a prophet. But I think she did.

Then Elijah called to her, "Bring me, I pray thee, a morsel of bread in thine hand." (1 Kings 17:11.) The widow, in humble testimony, declared, "As the Lord thy God liveth, I have not a cake, but an handful of meal in a barrel, and a little oil in a cruse [jar]: and, behold, I am gathering two sticks, that I may go in and dress it for me and my son, that we may eat it, and die." (1 Kings 17:12.)

Then came the greater test. The widow had only enough meal and oil to prepare a small cake that she and her son would divide. Then there was nothing more, no hope of anything else. She had consigned herself to the fact that that would be their last meal and then death would come. Then Elijah bore testimony to the widow: "Fear not; go and do as thou hast said: but make me thereof a little cake first, and bring it unto me, and after make for thee and for thy son." (1 Kings 17:13.)

The widow knew that what Elijah asked was impossible. There would be no meal left after she made a cake for him, but Elijah said, "Thus saith the Lord God of Israel, The barrel of meal shall not waste, neither shall the cruse of oil fail, until the day that the Lord sendeth rain upon the earth." (1 Kings 17:14.)

This wonderful widow was simply obedient: "She went and did according to the saying of Elijah: and she and he, and her house, did eat many days." (1 Kings 17:15.) We are not sure how long a period "many days" was, but it was sufficient to test the Lord. She simply laid all she had, to her last meal, on the altar of God. It would not have mattered, I think, whether Elijah had promised her that the barrel would not waste nor the cruse fail. She knew he was a prophet of God and would have submitted totally to his needs.

Then came the miracle: "The barrel of meal wasted not, neither did the cruse of oil fail, according to the word of the Lord, which he spake by Elijah." (1 Kings 17:16.) This is the key, "the word of the Lord." Whenever we put our absolute trust in God, our spiritual barrels and our cruses fail not. We can never get out of the Lord's debt. We owe him for all we are, for everything we may become, and for our very lives.

Whenever we are obedient, additional blessings come to us. Soon after Elijah had moved in with the widow, "the son of the woman, the mistress of the house, fell sick and his sickness was so sore, that there was no breath left in him." (1 Kings 17:17.) The widow went to Elijah and confessed her sins, thinking that her son's death might have been punishment from God through Elijah.

This beloved prophet said to the woman, "Give me thy son. And he took [the son] out of her bosom, and carried him up into a loft where he abode, and laid him upon his own bed." (1 Kings 17:18.) Elijah was living under the most humble of circumstances, in the loft. The prophets in ancient as well as modern times have always been men of great humility who have eaten and lived in the most humble conditions.

Elijah "cried unto the Lord, and said, O Lord my God, hast thou also brought evil upon the widow with whom I sojourn?" (1 Kings 17:20.) Even Elijah did not understand why the son was sick, but he had absolute confidence that God would heal him. Continuing his prayer he said, "O Lord my God, I pray thee, let this child's soul come into him again. And the Lord heard the voice of Elijah; and the soul of the child came into him again." (1 Kings 17:20-21.)

Then "Elijah took the child, and brought him down out of the chamber into the house, and delivered him unto his mother: and Elijah said, See, thy son liveth." The widow once again affirmed her testimony: "Now by this I know that thou art a man of God, and that the word of the Lord in thy mouth is truth." (1 Kings 17:23–24.)

The word of the Lord in the mouth of his holy prophets is truth, and you should obey that truth. Always trust in the prophets and be prepared to accept their inspired counsel and direction. Although the Aaronic Priesthood is sometimes referred to as the lesser priesthood, it still holds great power.

You need not be a prophet to fulfill your priesthood responsibilities, to perform miracles, or to be a great influence for good.

Remember that the priesthood is the authority to act in God's name. Outside of The Church of Jesus Christ of Latter-day Saints, there is no legal authority from God. The most humble, worthy deacon has more authority in the kingdom of God than all the ministers of religion or rulers of nations.

Be faithful, and trust in and follow the prophets of God. Develop faith like that of the widow, so that anything the prophet asks you to do, you will do. Follow his counsel and be obedient in his direction. By doing so, you will receive blessings that will exceed all that you have dreamed. I promise you that as you are obedient, your spiritual barrel will not waste, nor will your cruse fail.

Chapter 13

Jonah

There is a short book in the Old Testament about an unusual servant of the Lord. His name was Jonah. This prophet was of Gath-hepher in Zebulon. He reigned under Jeroboam II, whose success in restoring the ancient boundaries of Israel he predicted. The present book of Jonah does not claim to be from the hand of the prophet. It does, however, describe an episode in his life.

The word of the Lord came to Jonah: "Arise, go to Nineveh, that great city, and cry against it; for their wickedness is come up before me." (Jonah 1:2.)

But instead, Jonah ran from his responsibility. He found a ship going to Tarshish, so he paid the fare and got on board, hoping to flee from the Lord. Then the Lord sent a great wind into the sea. The waves were so high that the sailors feared that the ship would be wrecked. But this life-threatening storm did not awaken Jonah. He had gone into the ship, where he lay fast asleep.

The crew had been through great storms before but apparently none to compare with this one. They even began to throw goods into the sea to lighten the ship, and all of them began to pray. Mariners in ancient days as well as those in our nation's history were a rugged lot. For them to pray, conditions would have to be serious indeed.

The captain came to Jonah and said, "What meanest thou, O sleeper?" (I suppose that *sleeper* is a good word to describe those in the Church who turn away from their duty.) Then he said to Jonah, "Arise, call upon thy God, if so be that God will think upon us, that we perish not." (Jonah 1:6.)

Jonah must have had some reputation of being a righteous man. Perhaps the captain had reason to believe that Jonah had some persuasive power with the Lord. The sailors decided to cast lots so they would know who was the cause of the storm. The lot fell upon Jonah.

The men then said, "Tell us we pray thee, for whose cause this evil is upon us; what is thine occupation? and whence comest thou? and of what people art thou?" They apparently felt that by knowing a little more about Jonah, they might better determine if he was the cause of the problem.

Jonah said that he was a Hebrew who feared the Lord, the God of Heaven, who made the sea and the dry land. There seems to be some dialogue missing, for the scripture states that "the men knew that he fled from the presence of the Lord." They were afraid, and asked him, "Why hast thou done this?"

"Then said they unto him, what shall we do unto thee that the sea may be calm before us? for the sea wrought, and was tempestuous." We learn a lot from Jonah's answer—he was no coward: "Take me up, and cast me forth into the sea; so shall the sea be calm unto you: for I know that for my sake this great tempest is upon you." (Jonah 2:10-12.) Jonah was willing to give his life for the crew on the boat. The Lord has said, "Greater love hath no man than this, that he lay down his life for his friends." (John 15:13.)

We have to reason that Jonah had a great deal of character but simply lacked the necessary faith in Christ. The men rowed hard to bring the boat to land, but they could not. Then these men cried to the Lord that they would not perish for this man's life. They recognized that the Lord had done as he pleased.

"So they took up Jonah, and cast him forth into the sea: and the sea ceased from her raging." (Jonah 1:15.) The Lord had prepared a great fish to swallow Jonah. Jonah fully expected to be drowned in the depth of the sea. But this was not what the Lord had in mind. Jonah was in the belly of the fish three days and three nights. It would be impossible to conceive of the terror Jonah went through during this time. He may have slept on the ship during the storm, but think how he must have felt knowing every moment that his life could come to a violent end.

It appears that this stubborn man of great character finally conceded; he prayed to the Lord out of the belly of the fish. This is a wonderful example, showing us that no matter where we are, in the deepest crevice on this globe, in the deepest part of the darkest forest, on the loneliest desert, or on the highest mountain, God's loving care can encircle us. To the wicked, it is a message that there is no place to hide from God and his justice.

After three incomprehensible days of terror, the Lord spoke to the fish, "and it vomited out Jonah upon the dry land."

The word of the Lord came the second time to a submissive Jonah: "Arise and go to Nineveh, that great city, and preach unto it the preaching that I bid thee." (Jonah 3:2.) Jonah arose and went to Nineveh according to the word of the Lord. This was a large city—it took three days to travel through it. "And Jonah began to enter into the city a day's journey, and he said, Yet forty days and Nineveh shall be overthrown." (Jonah 3:4.)

Jonah must have been a powerful preacher. He must have been endowed with the Spirit, for the people believed that he spoke for God. They proclaimed a fast and put on sackcloth, from the greatest to the least of them. Jonah's preaching and his powerful words penetrated everyone. Even the king of Nineveh "arose from his throne, and he laid his robe from

him, and covered him with sackcloth, and sat in ashes." And
the king sent out a proclamation that "neither man nor beast,
herd nor flock, taste any thing: let them not feed, nor drink
water: but let man and beast be covered with sackcloth, and
cry mightily unto God: yea, let them turn every one from his
evil way, and from the violence that is in their hands." (Jonah
3:6–8.)

We have had some marvelous preachers in ancient and
modern days, but Jonah must have been one of the greatest.
He must have spoken with such spiritual eloquence and force-
fulness that all the inhabitants repented as directed by the
king. For he said, "Who can tell if God will turn and repent,
and turn away from his fierce anger, that we perish not?"
(Jonah 3:9.) It is evident that the people were convinced that
Jonah was a representative of the Lord.

"And God saw their works, that they turned from their
evil way; and God repented of the evil, that he said that he
would do unto them and did it not." (Jonah 3:10.)

Jonah, who had been ever so close to death, who had
had a harrowing experience like none before nor since, then
called another time upon the Lord: "Take I beseech thee, my
life from me; for it is better for me to die than to live."

The Lord questioned whether Jonah had a right to be
angry because the people were spared. We would suspect
that Jonah would have humbled himself to the dust because
of what the Lord had done to touch the hearts of the people
through him. But Jonah did not. Apparently he felt that the
Lord should have destroyed this people who had once been
so wicked, and because he had not, Jonah was ready to die.

"Then Jonah went out of the city, and sat on the east side
of the city, and there made him a booth [shelter] and sat
under it in the shadow, till he might see what would become
of the city." Now the Lord loved his servant Jonah. He knew
Jonah better than Jonah knew himself. He knew what troubled
his servant, and he prepared a great teaching experience for
him: "And the Lord God prepared a gourd, and made it to
come up over Jonah, that it might be a shadow [to provide

shade] over his head, to deliver him from his grief. So Jonah was exceeding glad of the gourd. But God prepared a worm when the morning rose the next day, and it smote the gourd that it withered. . . . The Lord prepared a vehement east wind; and the sun beat upon the head of Jonah, that he fainted, and wished in himself to die, and said, It is better for me to die than to live." (Jonah 4:6–8.)

I have met people like Jonah who have more talent and ability in their little finger than some of us do in our whole body, but they lack charity, the pure love of Christ. What a blessing it is to have implicit trust in the Lord. I have known people who are angry with the Lord for the conditions in their lives. But life is not meant to be easy. President Harold B. Lee said we would be tested every month of our lives. Is this reason to be angry at the Lord, or should we love him even more? The Lord loves whom he chastens.

The Lord knew Jonah's heart, and he said, "Doest thou well to be angry for the gourd?" Then said the Lord, "Thou hast had pity on the gourd, for the which thou hast not laboured, neither madest it grow; which came up in a night, and perished in a night: and should not I spare Nineveh, that great city, wherein are more than sixscore thousand persons?" (Jonah 4:9–11.)

Jonah must have been pure and clean or the Lord would not have called him to serve. He must have had a powerful voice for righteousness, because the people listened. He must have had a fearlessness that took him into the valley of death, and he must have been strong. But Jonah's problem was a lack of faith in Christ and charity for others. Most of us would have been humbled to the dust when the people repented. We would have shed great tears of joy that the city had been spared. But Jonah was angry.

We must have love for every soul with whom we labor. President Harold B. Lee said, "I came to a night some years ago upon my bed, that if I would be worthy of the high place to which I had been called I must love and forgive every soul that walks the earth."

Your ministry as an Aaronic Priesthood bearer is to love and serve with a forgiving heart. Use the talents God has given you. Labor with success as did Jonah, for you can learn much from this Old Testament prophet. But use your talents with the pure love of Christ to bring souls into God's kingdom. Your mission is to go wherever the Lord chooses to send you and to labor with all the energy of your soul in an attitude of love.

Chapter 14

The Mormon
Pioneers

The pioneers left us a rich legacy of sacrifice, integrity, work, loyalty, and, above all else, faith in Christ. The trek westward provided the early church with an experience that purged and prepared the Saints and laid a foundation of faith upon which the mightiest edifice ever built would be erected. This church is that monument. There are now over six million members of the Church who have been blessed and endowed with character and integrity through the monumental sacrifice and devotion of the pioneers.

A verse by Ted Olsen describes well the courage and perseverance of the pioneers:

> Ninety and nine are with dreams content;
> But the hope of a world made new
> Is the hundredth man who is grimly bent
> On making the dream come true.
>
> (*Muir's Thesaurus of Truths*, p. 16.)

Beginning February 4, 1846, the first of the pioneers left Nauvoo and crossed the frozen Mississippi River. That alone was a miracle. I have discussed the freezing of the Mississippi with modern residents of Nauvoo, who say that rarely does the Mississippi freeze over.

It would be a trial even to us, with our motor homes, trailers, and modern travel conveniences, to be displaced in mid-February. The cold is an awesome foe. It is difficult for us to comprehend the faith necessary to load a covered wagon and leave all else behind.

One account states: "The trail of the Mormon pioneers across Iowa and the hard winter at Winter Quarters became the church's vale of tears, with mud, cold, rain and snow combining with the primitive living conditions, and exacting a terrible toll of illness and death. The Mormon Trail was marked with lonesome graves, 600—mostly children alone— dying at Winter Quarters. The Iowa mud often bogged down the wagons to the axles. Some days only a quarter of a mile of progress would be made all day, and then with wagons double-teamed." (LDS Church Public Communications Department News Release, July 7, 1973, from Norman R. Bowen.)

There is really no way to understand in the smallest degree the trials and suffering that accompanied that special generation of Saints. We can honor the pioneers for what they did, but only those who went through it will ever truly know the extent to which they suffered.

I believe our present generation has been preserved and held in reserve for this day, but I also know that those who made the westward exodus were a magnificent, faith-filled generation for a time when the restored gospel required physically more than most of us will ever know.

We think of trails through ice, snow, rain, and mud, across prairies, over mountains, through rivers, in the most savage conditions, and we melt to tears at the bravery of the pioneers. Imagine feeling so cold, being so frozen, that even an attempt to remove stockings pulls off layers of flesh. Try to comprehend the chill of the northern winds bringing sleet, rain, and snow upon a humble, quiet, holy people who wanted nothing more than to worship their God in peace. They provided no danger, no threat. They desired no retribution but only a quiet, sacred place where they would be left alone with their faith. They had no thought to leave Nauvoo, especially in the winter. They were building a wonderful community on a recovered swamp on a bend of the great Mississippi River. Now they were driven ruthlessly out of their homes to a desperate, bleak prairie of ice and snow. But they went.

Consider the lack of clothing, the need for food, a little shelter, a resting place. The winter storms took their toll and exacted the best blood of that generation. Newborn babies were laid in shallow graves. How often these scenes were repeated few know.

With the spring came the dust and the hot sun. Blisters and sweat replaced the frosted and frozen feet. Every day the toiling work continued—up and down, over and across, always looking forward. Many made the entire journey on foot.

Some sacrifices were so obscure that they may never be known, but the collective suffering, the endowment more precious than gold, will never be forgotton by many of us who follow.

The covered wagons were followed by the handcart companies, which hold a special place in my heart. The only power to make the handcarts roll was the man, woman, or child who pushed or pulled. When the strength to push or pull was exhausted, there was no horse or ox to pull. Men and women became beasts of burden. They endured pain and suffering beyond belief. And as an Aaronic Priesthood holder, you must develop spiritual strength even beyond that of the pioneers.

Three handcart companies preceded the Willie and Martin handcart companies. They left on June 9, 11, and 23, 1856, and lost respectively one, seven, and no lives in making their brave trek. The Willie handcart company commenced on July 15, 1856, with about 500 souls, and 66 were buried along the old Mormon Trail. There were 575 in the Edward Martin company, and 135 of them were rescued by an Eternal God who must have taken them home in mercy. What would the feelings of an Eternal Parent be to watch his children suffering and freezing?

Their faith in the God of heaven gave them hope. Those who died in this enormous effort, I believe, were taken into the celestial kingdom. It seems to me that those who gave their last breath during the pioneer exodus were secure in their eternal blessings.

Gustive O. Larson described the first two companies to enter the Great Salt Lake Valley:

> They were met near the mouth of Emigration Canyon by President Brigham Young, Heber C. Kimball, and Daniel H. Wells. There was also a band and a military escort. Men, women, and children thronged out to see and welcome the first handcart companies. The number increased until the living tide lined and thronged South Temple. An eyewitness wrote "As they came down the bench you could scarcely see them for the dust. When they entered the City the folks came running from every quarter to get a glimpse of the long-looked-for handcarts. . . . I shall never forget the feeling that ran through my whole system as I caught first sight of them. The first handcart was drawn by a man and his wife. They had a little flag on it, on which were the words, 'Our President, may the unity of the Saints ever show the wisdom of his counsels.'" (Gustive O. Larson, *Mormon Handcart Story* [Salt Lake City: Deseret Book Company, 1956], pp.15-16.)

As you can imagine, President Brigham's heart must have swelled as wide as the valley and his eyes brimmed with tears as he read this sign, which represented their loyalty and the greatness of their faith. Then, "the next handcart was drawn by three young women. The tears ran down the cheeks of many a man who you would have thought would not, could not, shed a tear." (Ibid., p.16.)

Clarence F. Scharer stated in the *American School Board Journal*: "The real qualities of leadership are found in those who are willing to sacrifice for the sake of objectives great enough to demand their wholehearted allegiance. Simply holding a position of leadership does not make a man a leader. . . . If you would be a real leader, you must endure loneliness. . . . If you would be a real leader, you must endure weariness. . . . Leadership requires vision. A real leader ought to be able to foresee what his policies will do to the next generation. Vision must have hope and optimism in it. The past [generation] must push us—never pull us."

The pioneer generation furnished the push and the pull. We recall the costs to both life and limb of those who thus toiled. The Willie handcart company as they traveled up the Sweetwater River country had reduced their rations to average 10 ounces of flour a day. They reported: "We had not traveled far up the Sweetwater before the nights, which had gradually been getting colder since we left Laramie, became very severe. The mountains before us, as we approached nearer to them, revealed themselves to be mantled nearly to their base in snow, and tokens of a coming storm were discernible in the clouds which each day seemed to lower around us.

"Cold weather, scarcity of food, lassitude and fatigue from over-exertion, soon produced their effects. Our old and infirm people began to droop, and they no sooner lost spirit and courage than death's stamp could be traced upon their features. Life went out as smoothly as a lamp ceases to burn when the oil is gone. . . . Death was not long confined in its ravages to the old and infirm, but the young and naturally strong were among its victims. . . . Many a father pulled his cart, with his little children on it, until the day preceding his death."

Then these sad words were penned: "We travelled on in misery and sorrow day after day. . . . Finally we were overtaken by a snowstorm which the shrill wind blew furiously about us. The snow fell several inches deep as we travelled along, but we dared not stop, for we had a sixteen-mile journey to make, and short of it we could not get wood and water.

"As we were resting for a short time at noon a light wagon was driven into our camp from the west. Its occupants were Joseph A. Young and Stephen Taylor. They informed us that a train of supplies was on the way, and we might expect to meet it in a day or two. More welcome messengers never came from the courts of glory than these two young men were to us." (Leroy R. and Ann W. Hafen, *Handcarts to Zion* [Glendale: Arthur H. Clark Company, 1960], p. 102.)

Nor was it an easy task for those on the supply wagons. They faced the same snow, now over a foot deep. Captain Willie and a companion went in search of those who brought supplies. They were gone for three days. The only food remaining for those in the Willie company was a barrel of hard bread procured at Fort Laramie and the gaunt cattle.

The Martin company was in an even more precarious condition. A Sister Jackson recorded: "The male members of the company had become reduced in number by death and those who remained were so weak and emaciated by sickness, that on reaching the camping place at night, there were not sufficient men with strength enough to raise the poles and pitch the tents. The result was that we camped out with nothing but the vault of Heaven for a roof and the stars for companions. The night was bitterly cold. I sat down on a rock with one child in my lap and one on each side of me. In that condition I remained until morning." (Ibid., p. 112.)

John Bond recorded: "Deaths continued in the camp. Some died lying side by side with hands entwined. In other cases, they were found as it they had just offered a fervent prayer and their spirit had taken flight while in the act." (Ibid., p. 113.)

One of the most humble and touching stories is that of Samuel and Margaret Pucell and their two daughters Ellen and Maggie. The mother, Margaret, "became ill so she had to ride in the handcart part of the way. Her husband grew so weary and weakened from the lack of food that this additional burden caused him to slip and fall one day as he crossed a river. Having to travel in the cold, wintry weather with wet clothing he, too, became ill and died from hunger and exposure. His wife died five days later, leaving ten-year-old Ellen and fourteen-year-old Maggie orphans." Both the Pucell girls suffered badly from frozen feet and legs. "When shoes and stockings were removed from the girl's feet, the skin came off. Although Maggie's legs were frozen, she would not allow them to do more than scrape the flesh off the bones, but Ellen's were so bad they had to be amputated just below the knees." (Ibid., p. 138.) Surgery was performed with the rough implements of the day.

What a mission of mercy the wagon train sent by President Brigham Young proved to be. Other accounts have also been recorded. President David O. McKay, at the annual Relief Society Conference in 1947, talked of the criticism given by a teacher who commented that it was very unwise even to have permitted the Saints to cross the plains under such circumstances. President McKay said:

> Some sharp criticism of the Church and its leaders was being indulged in for permitting any company of converts to venture across the plains with no more supplies or protection than a handcart caravan afforded.
>
> An old man in the corner (and this was written by President William Palmer, who was present) sat silent and listened as long as he could stand it, then he arose and said things that no person who heard him will ever forget. His face was white with emotion, yet he spoke calmly, deliberately, but with great earnestness and sincerity.
>
> In substance the father above mentioned said, "I ask you to stop this criticism. You are discussing a matter you know nothing about. Cold historic facts mean nothing here, for they give no proper interpretation of the questions involved. Mistake to send the Handcart Company out so late in the season? Yes. But I was in that company and my wife was in it and Sister Nellie Unthank whom you have cited was there, too. We suffered beyond anything you can imagine and many died of exposure and starvation, but did you ever hear a survivor of that company utter a word of criticism? Not one of that company ever apostatized or left the Church, because everyone of

us came through with the absolute knowledge that God lives, for we became aquainted with him in our extremeties.

"I have pulled my handcart when I was so weak and weary from illness and lack of food that I could hardly put one foot ahead of the other. I have looked ahead and seen a patch of sand or a hill slope and I have said, I can go only that far and there I must give up, for I cannot pull the load through it." And a wife with a baby in her arms by his side! "I have gone on to that sand and when I reached it, the cart began pushing me. I have looked back many times to see who was pushing my cart, but my eyes saw no one. I knew then that the angels of God were there.

"Was I sorry that I chose to come by handcart? No. Neither then nor any minute of my life since. The price we paid to become aquainted with God was a privilege to pay, and I am thankful that I was privileged to come in the Martin Handcart Company." (David O. McKay, "Pioneer Women," *Relief Society Magazine*, January 1948, p. 8.)

President J. Reuben Clark wrote a moving tribute entitled "To Them of the Last Wagon." His great empathy and love for the pioneers is reflected in how he describes how it might have been for "those who trod after where those giants led . . . some in the fateful handcarts with their unexcelled devotion, heroism, and faith, all trickling forward in a never-failing, tiny stream, till they filled the valley they entered and then flowed out at the sides and ends, peopling this whole wilderness-waste which they [made fruitful], making it to fulfill the ancient prophecy that the desert should blossom as the rose.

"But back in the last wagon, not always could they see the brethren way out in the front, and the blue heaven was often shut out from their sight by heavy, dense clouds of the dust of the earth. Yet day after day, they of the last wagon pressed forward, worn and tired, footsore, sometimes almost disheartened, borne up by their faith that God loved them.

" . . . When the train moved forward in the early morning sun and the oxen with a swinging pull that almost broke the tongue got the last wagon on the move, the dust in the still morning air hung heavy over the ground, till when the last wagon swung into line, the dust was dense and suffocating. It covered that last wagon and all that was in it; it clung to clothes; it blackened faces, it filled eyes already sore, and ears. The wife, soon to be a mother, could hardly catch her breath."

I believe that President Clark understood much of what the pioneers went through. Like him, we should take time to ponder the importance of their sacrifice and to become more like them.

In the Gettysburg Address, President Abraham Lincoln said of the soldiers of the Civil War, "The world will little note nor long remember what we say here, but it will never forget what they did here." Those words apply also to the handcart companies.

I would like to pay special tribute to the handcart companies in a poem I have written entitled, "They All Came Through in Glory."

> In July's hot sun,
> The trek begun,
>   The handcart companies toiled.
> With oxen to goad,
> And heavy load,
>   Their faces strong and soiled,
> They built and tooled,
> They pushed and pulled,
>   Till wearily they fell.
> They toiled and sweat,
> Till dripping wet,
>   They bid the past farewell.
> Up and down,
> No golden crown,
>   The dust rose up in clouds.
> From early dawn,
> They toiled on,
>   The cold around them shrouds.

The very best
Continued west,
    With all they owned they came.
Proud men,
Greater then,
    Stripped of pride and shame.
But the trials grew,
The windstorms blew,
    Came soon the dreadful foe.
Ice and cold,
Testing young and old,
    In whiteness fell the snow.
After labored breath,
With night came death,
    Brave souls lay in the grave.
Free of greed,
They shared indeed,
    But more, their lives they gave.
Frostbite came
And made some lame,
    Others never walked again.
Laid to sleep,
In snow knee deep,
    The roughest, toughest of men.
At night's end,
Death was their friend,
    Nor breathed they evermore.
Relief had come,
Life was done,
    Swept to an eternal shore.

Those still spared,
Less well they fared,
    For the crucible was fired white.
They wept and froze,
In their tattered clothes.
    Angels blessed them through the night.
Food grew scarce,
Life more sparse,
    A moment seemed like a life.

Yet they lost not faith
While fearing death
       Of daughter, son, or wife.
With rags wrapped 'round,
Their feet were bound,
       The penetrating cold still chilled.
The wolves came too
And dug graves through,
       Their starving stomachs filled.
Then from far away
Came help that day,
       With men, wagons, and supplies.
And great tears shed,
Over a loaf of bread,
       While brave rescuers wiped their eyes.

Now saw they light,
Through darkest night,
       For the caring brethren came.
Westward they streamed,
As they had dreamed,
       Came forth the bold and lame.
Through mountains steep
Where snow drifts deep,
       Their goal was almost reached.
Soon their valley home,
Under heaven's dome,
       Lay before them on deserts bleached.
To the valley floor,
Through the open door,
       To loving homes they came.
The pudding and bread,
To souls almost dead,
       Was as manna to their frame.
And now the years
Have dried the tears,
       Of the pioneer stories we tell.
Let us not forget
The trials they met
       Were the bitterest tests of hell.

> For their faith proved true,
> For me and you,
>   And they all came through in glory.
> The heart doth melt
> For the tests they felt,
>   In the brave pioneer handcart story.

I love the pioneers. I love this great church. I am grateful for my faith. I hope someday to kneel at the feet of those who laid their all, including their lives, on the altar of God. May we be an equally sterling generation of faith and devotion. As an Aaronic Priesthood bearer, you have a solemn obligation to be as fearless in facing trials as the pioneers. In fact, you must exceed them in faith, for days of great testing are ahead. Prepare yourself physically, mentally, and spiritually to serve the Lord. Keep yourself morally clean. Have faith in Christ and trust in God and prepare to do their work, which I testify is the most glorious, most precious, and most challenging of any work on the face of the earth. Prove yourself worthy of our noble and illustrious pioneer heritage.

Index

behavior when assisting
with, 56
Samuel the Lamanite, 65
Scharer, Clarence F., 87–88
Schmitt, Neil, 43–44
Service: is blessing, not burden, viii; as purpose of
priesthood, 8; in commemoration of priesthood restoration, 8; in priesthood quorum, 14; spiritual
experiences accompanying,
20; deep joy of, 34; is syn-
onymous with work, 36;
reactivation as, 46
Smith, Joseph, 3–4; 23; 61
Smith, Joseph F., 22–23
Spirituality, feelings of, 20
Swearing, 51
Swimming hole, race to jump
into, 44

Talmage, James E., 4–5
Temple marriage, working
toward, 53
Temptation: power to resist,
12; succumbing to, 69–71;
importance of resisting,
71–72

Testimony, importance of gain-
ing, 23
Thief: father labels boy as,
10–11
Tire needing fixing, boy prays
about, 27–28

Uriah, 69–70

Vandalism, 51–52

Weak things made strong,
17–18
Welfare farm, working on,
33–34, 36
Widow: feeds Elijah, 74–75;
son of, dies, 76
Widtsoe, John, 24
Willie handcart company,
88–89
Woodruff, Wilford, 4
Word of Wisdom, 51, 57
Work: necessity of, 36–37;
around home, 37–38; is
essential to maturity, 38
Worthiness, maintaining, 57

Youth programs, increased
priesthood emphasis in, 22